His Eminence

Roger Cardinal Mahony

humbly asks the Holy Father

Pope John Paul II

to bestow an Apostolic Blessing
on the staff and readers of the archdiocesan newspaper

The Tidings

to commemorate the centennial of its establishment
1895 ~   ~ 1995

SS.mus Dominus Apostolicam Benedictionem concedit.
Ex Aedibus Vaticanis die 2. IX. 1994

+ Oscar Rizzato

Archiepiscopus
Eleemosynarius Apostolicus

A Centennial History of

TIDINGS

Msgr. Francis J. Weber

Saint Francis Historical Society
1995

A Centennial History of the Tidings

Printed by Kimberly Press, Inc.
Santa Barbara

Library of Congress Cataloging-in-Publication Data

Weber, Francis J.
    A centennial history of the Tidings / Francis J. Weber.
      p.   cm.
    Includes bibliographical references.
    ISBN: 0-87461-923-8 (cloth)
    ISBN: 0-87461-924-6 (paper)
    1. Tidings – History. 2. Catholic Church. Archdiocese of Los
Angeles (Calif.) – History. 3. Catholic Church – California – Los
Angeles Region – History. 4. Los Angeles Region (Calif.) – Church
history. I. Title.
    BX1418.L7W43 1995
    282' .7949'05–dc20

Table of Contents

Preface

In a speech given to the Catholic Press Association at Baltimore in 1962, Msgr. John Tracy Ellis proposed that "serious thought be given to sponsoring a scholarly history of the Catholic press in the United States." Unhappily, that suggestion died aborning. In more recent times, others have joined in calling for a history of the Catholic press, noting that "a diocesan newspaper is the diary of God's people as they make their way along the pathway to salvation."

This history of *The Tidings*, prepared in anticipation of the paper's centennial on June 29, 1995, is a response to Ellis and others who have rightly considered local Catholic newspapers as vital to the life of the local diocesan family. *The Tidings* does indeed have a history worth recalling. In all its 5,197 issues, the oldest continuously published Catholic newspaper on the west coast of America has never missed a deadline, disappointed its readers or betrayed the trust of its publisher.

A clear conscience goes hand-in-hand with an exact understanding of our individual roles. Hence, publications are not merely informative, but formative as well; that is, of vital educational value. No one can deny that the Catholic press is both a means for expressing public opinion and an avenue for shaping and educating it, and even at times for warping it.

No less a personage than Thomas Jefferson once observed that "were it left to me to decide whether we should have a government without newspapers or newspapers without a government, I should not hesitate a moment to prefer the latter."

In its edition for July 28, 1990, the Los Angeles *Daily News* quoted Owen McGovern of the Catholic Press Association as saying that *The Tidings* has been at the forefront of most of the changes involving Catholic newspapers over the years." "To say *The Tidings* has been innovative is an understatement," he said. "It is impressive that the Archdiocese has had faith in the publication after all these years. Bishops come and change, yet the Los Angeles Archdiocese has committed itself to a newspaper for ninety-five years."

That *The Tidings* has been esteemed, even by its sister publications of other persuasions, is obvious too. Rabbi Yale B. Butler, editor of *The B'nai B'rith Messenger*, said that *The Tidings* has done a good job serving the Catholic community. "Over the years, we have worked together on various civic projects to try to solve some of the problems in the community, such as disease and poverty."

It was this writer's privilege to serve as interim editor of *The Tidings* for fifteen issues (May 18 through August 24, 1990). That experience was the culmination of a love affair dating back to the mid-1940s. To have held the tiller of this "Grand Old Lady of the Catholic Press" in my hand, even for a few weeks, was a most fulfilling experience.

The Lord has endowed the years of my priestly ministry with abundant blessings, allowing me to be archivist, historian, professor, bookseller, author, bibliographer and even pastor. But the title I cherish above all others is that of interim editor for *The Tidings*. And that explains why it's been so much fun preparing this history.

The author is indebted to Gladys Posakony and Alphonse Antczak, both of whom read the manuscript and offered innumerable suggestions, together with Ginny Brophy-Jenski who typed the manuscript.

Pre-Cursors to the Catholic Tidings, 1858-1905

Since 1858, the journalistic needs of Catholics in California had been well served by *The Monitor* which was founded at San Francisco by James Marks, Patrick J. Thomas and James Hamill. Throughout the early years, James Hamill dedicated the journal to publishing "all domestic and foreign newsworthy events of interest to the Catholics of California."

According to the San Francisco *Herald*, *The Monitor's* early editorials exhibited talent "far above the standard which generally obtains in California" and merited the support of "our Roman Catholic population, who, in point of intelligence, worth and numbers, require a representative through the press of their sentiments."

Archbishop Alemany and several of his priests purchased a half interest in the paper on December 27, 1876, and the issue of April 7, 1877 carried the following letter signed by the Archbishop of San Francisco: "Right Rev. Bishop Amat, of Monterey- Los Angeles, Right Rev. Bishop O'Connell, of Marysville and myself take pleasure in declaring to our respective flocks that we beg to avail ourselves of your useful and ably edited *Monitor* as our official organ."

During most of the next two decades, there was a regular column in *The Monitor* which reported most of the events of a Catholic nature that occurred in the Diocese of Monterey-Los Angeles. Though a large number of people in Southern California subscribed to *The Monitor*, many of the area's leading Catholics felt the need for newspaper more oriented to the needs of the southland..

With the public endorsement of Bishop Francis Mora, James McGee secured financial underwriting in mid-1888 for the *California Catholic*. Initially, the newspaper was quite successful and by the end of the year, the publication had attracted national attention. An editorial in the Indianapolis *New Record* referred to the "Church of Los Angeles" as "full of life and activity" sustaining "a vigorous, enterprising, bright-looking newspaper, the *California Catholic*." Issued under the management of W. D. S. Harrington and Father Charles Tanquerey, the paper perdured for about two years before discontinuing publication under the editorship of John J. Bodkin.

A Portuguese publication, *O Amigos dos Catolicos*, was established at Irvington, by Manuel Fernandez and Jose Tavares. After a year the paper passed under lay control and was moved to Pleasanton. A subsequent movement to organize a Catholic Press Association in 1889 likewise failed because some of the strong secular papers "did not take kindly to the idea, presumably for the reason that they feared the weak ones would be helped thereby, and thus, possibly curtail their own circulation."

About the year 1890, Bishop Mora, anxious to have a diocesan paper, asked Joseph Mesmer whether such a venture could be self-supporting. Mesmer called a meeting of the city's Catholic merchants and, with the support of Edward J. Robertson and Isidore B. Dockweiler, agreed to form a stock company. With $10,000 subscribed capital, the trio launched the southland's third Catholic newspaper.

The first edition of the *Cause* appeared on October 4, 1890; however, trouble soon developed. Even though the proprietors purchased no plant, preferring to have their printing done by contract, the paper was in serious trouble within fifteen months. Bankruptcy brought about the publication's demise in 1892. Shortly after disbanding the *Cause*, a Mr. Harrington undertook to resurrect the enterprise, changing the name of the publication to *The Voice*. The paper was published for a short period but Catholic support proved too weak to sustain their activities.

American Protective Association - 1890s

A mong the more compelling reasons for establishing a Catholic newspaper in Southern California during the 1890s was the presence of the exceedingly powerful and virtriolic American Protective Association. Founded by Henry F. Bowers in the late 1880s, the A.P.A. attempted to combat alleged "attacks by the Catholic Church on the public schools and other American institutions."

Members were required "at all times to place the political positions of the government in the hands of Protestants to the entire exclusion of the Roman Catholics." In its early years, the A.P.A. was remarkably successful and, by 1894, its branches throughout the nation had elected no less than twenty members to the United States Congress.

Actually a recrudescence of the worse doctrines of the Know-Nothing Party of the 1850s, the A.P.A. harbored a special hostility to foreign-born citizens of a "Catholic persuasion" whom they wanted banned from all public offices. Orestes Brownson pointed out that the A.P.A.'s opposition to foreigners was "selective, insofar as members did not oppose Protestant Germans, Protestant Englishmen, Protestant Scotsmen, or even Protestant Irishmen. They were really opposed only to Catholic foreigners." Practically all city and county government positions of importance in Los Angeles, San Diego, Pasadena, Redlands and Riverside were held by members of the A.P.A. or people favored by that organization. By 1894, religious intolerance against Catholics had reached fever-pitch.

One knowledgeable writer claimed that during its years of dominancy, "the A.P.A. maintained a persecution of Catholics in Southern California unequalled in the history of any free country."

Interestingly, little reference was made to this anti-Catholic bias in the pages of the local secular press which was apprehensive about losing advertising patronage. The Bishop of Monterey-Los Angeles, a central object of vilifications because of his foreign birth and halting use of English, was mostly ignored in contemporary newspaper coverage.

In his memoirs, Patrick W. Croake, founder of the *Catholic Tidings*, recalled that "in those earlier days of religious bigotry, continued persecution finally resulted in welding together into one solid mass, not only the people of our common faith, but the friends of liberty of all denominations and of none."

The great opponent of the A.P.A. in California was Father Peter C. Yorke of San Francisco. In an unending barrage of public appearances, heated debates and forceful newspaper articles, Yorke became the nationally recognized debunker of the A.P.A. In 1896, the San Francisco priest published his book entitled *The Yorke-Wendte Discussion on the Primacy of the Pope, Church and State*, which was circulated widely in the southland. Patrick Croake dreamed of establishing a newspaper for Southern California that would bring to the local scene the writings of Peter Yorke.

Though Croake's tactics were eventually successful, there were many dark days. Croake once recalled that even after the launching of the *Catholic Tidings*, "several lay committees waited upon me to advocate the demise of the paper. They claimed that it caused the A.P.A. leaders to be more antagonistic than before. Many Catholic merchandisers were afraid to advertise." But Patrick Croake and his *Catholic Tidings* ultimately turned the tide. The launching of the newspaper marked the beginning of the end for the American Protective Association in the Diocese of Monterey-Los Angeles.

Diocese of Monterey-Los Angeles in 1895

By anyone's calculations, the challenge of inaugurating a Catholic newspaper in the Southern California of 1895 was indeed a formidable one. Few journalistic enterprises faced greater obstacles.

In 1895, the Diocese of Monterey-Los Angeles was bounded by Arizona on the east, the Pacific Ocean on the west, Baja California on the south and the 37th degree of latitude and Mono county in the north. Its territory embraced all or portions of Merced, Santa Clara, Santa Cruz, Fresno, Inyo, Kern, Los Angeles, Monterey, Orange, Riverside, San Benito, San Bernardino, San Luis Obispo, Santa Barbara, Tulare and Ventura counties, an area of approximately 75,984 square miles.

In the southern part of the diocese, there were vast areas of uncultivated land with few settlements and churches. Much of the territory had so few advantages of soil and climate that it depended on the more prolific districts to the north and east.

All things considered, the future of the Church in the area was anything but attractive. A prominent ecclesial historian, after surveying the scene, wrote that "had there been an open contest among the American clergy for the position as bishop in the Diocese of Monterey-Los Angeles, there would have been few if any applicants."

The approximately 50,000 Catholics in the diocese were being cared for spiritually by seventy-six priests in forty-two parishes, thirty-one parochial churches, and thirty-one stations. There was a total enrollment of 4,443 youngsters in the eleven academies and thirteen parochial schools scattered across a jurisdiction larger than many eastern states. Indeed, statistically, the Diocese of Monterey-Los Angeles was larger in territory and smaller in Catholics than any other district in the entire United States.

A clerical visitor from New York had this to say in a letter to a confrere: "The Diocese of Monterey-Los Angeles could best be described as a step-child of the American Church. Its foreign-born bishop is a good and pious man who speaks miserable English and appears to be desperate for clergymen to staff his scattered flock."

Surely the future must have looked bleak to Bishop Francis Mora. He had only one seminarian, his financial spread-sheet abounded in red ink and his health was broken and unsure. Added to those problems was the widespread religious intolerance of everything Catholic, a virus actively spread by the American Protective Association.

Bishop Mora had asked the Sacred Congregation of Propaganda Fide in early 1893 to accept his resignation. Miecislas Cardinal Ledochowski counter- proposed that Mora accept a coadjutor and, early the following year, Father George T. Montgomery, a priest of the Archdiocese of San Francisco, was named to the position.

Soon after the arrival of Montgomery, Mora took an extended vacation to Europe where he hoped to regain his health. When it became evident that he would not appreciably recover, he submitted his resignation to Pope Leo XIII.

The greatest theatrical productions are those produced without or apart from elaborate or costly staging. Surely there was little or no "staging" for *The Tidings* when it appeared in 1895!

Patrick Croake the Founder, 1895

Successful newspapers reflect the personality of their editors and surely that was true of Patrick Croake (1864-1958), the venerable and beloved "founder" of the *Catholic Tidings*.

Born in Utica, New York of Irish parents, Patrick studied at Saint Patrick's Academy in Chicago and later took graduate courses in journalism. He came west in 1889 to gather material for a descriptive booklet about the states of Washington and Oregon.

Several years later, Croake settled in San Diego, where he became involved in the newspaper trade. He was active in the Junipero Serra Club and it was there that he learned there was no journalistic proponent of the Catholic cause in Los Angeles.

Croake solicited the assistance of two friends, James Connolly, a retired sea captain and a writer of some distinction, and Kate Murphy, a typographer for the San Diego *Union*, to join him in establishing a newspaper in Los Angeles. In a subsequent memoir , Croake described Connolly as "wielding a trenchant pen during the four months of his incumbency."

With a loan of $500 from Connolly, Croake rented an upstairs office at 258 New High Street. The editor admitted that "it was tough sledding at first." The landlord, reportedly the richest man in the city, threatened eviction if the rent wasn't promptly paid on the first day of the month.

The first issue of the *Catholic Tidings* appeared on June 29, 1895 and ever so gradually, local professional and working people rallied to the support of the struggling journal.

Croake didn't find it an easy chore selling the idea of a Catholic newspaper. Subscribers were difficult to obtain, many of them recalling how earlier Catholic newspapers had gone into bankruptcy. And within months, both Connolly and Murphy had returned to their earlier work in San Diego, leaving Croake to carry on the work with the aid of his wife, the former Marie Russell, whom he had married in 1890.

An interesting footnote to those early days was the personage of the first "printer's devil" for the newspaper. Though Croake couldn't pay much for an assistant, he was able to secure the services of a youngster rather reasonably, one Eugene Biscailuz, who proved to be a "willing and efficient worker." Croake remained at the helm of the *Catholic Tidings* and its successor, *The Tidings*, until 1899. He had early on decided that the paper would not pass out of his hands until he found someone willing and able to assure its continuity. That individual surfaced in 1899, in the person of John Bodkin, a school teacher from San Gabriel

In an interview with Croake conducted in 1949, Sister Mary St. Joseph Feickert described him as a person "endowed with a strong, determined character, a deep religious conviction, great energy and the strictest integrity." After leaving *The Tidings*, Croake became active in the real estate business where he accumulated a modest fortune. Unfortunately, he lost everything in the Great Depression.

In the Centennial issue of *The Tidings*, Patrick Croake recalled his days as founder of *The Tidings*. It was a precious memoir which told much more about the man than it did about the paper he launched.

Inaugural Issue of the Newspaper - 1895

L ate one June night in 1895, Patrick Croake trudged down Main
Street from McElheney's Print Shop to the Post Office at Main
and Winston Streets. Slung over his shoulder was a hefty mail bag
containing a thousand copies of the Volume One, Number One issue
of the *Catholic Tidings*.

The inaugural issue containing eight pages with nine
advertisements, sold for 5¢. Begun bravely on a total capital of $400,
it boldly announced a "greeting" to Catholics in the Diocese of
Monterey- Los Angeles, promising to publish all "the available
Catholic news of the day."

The first page featured the text of a lecture on "Religion, Labor
and Capital" that had been given at the Los Angeles Theatre four
days earlier by Coadjutor Bishop George T. Montgomery. Readers
were told that Senator Reginaldo Del Valle had introduced the
speaker for the occasion.

Elsewhere in its first issue, the *Catholic Tidings* carried several
articles advocating women's equality. There were also essays on
"The Faith of Our Fathers" and "Reformers in the Cause of
Temperance."

In the news columns, the editor reported that Bishop
Montgomery had conferred diplomas at commencement exercises
for Saint Joseph School's. The program for that occasion included
recitation of The Dying Newsboy" by Miss Lissie Bissen, followed
with a "Farewell" by Emma Mulhardt. There were other essays on
such topics as "What Our Youth Read," wherein the writer deplored
the wide popularity of fictional works by Rider Haggard.

An editorial on page four expressed the hope that, despite its
modest circulation, the *Catholic Tidings* would rapidly grow and thus
be able to disseminate the truth of the Church: "From Monterey to

Mexico, from the sea to the Sierra, it will seek out every Catholic home, and strive to reach each Catholic heart."

There was a fairly good spread of national and world events mentioned in the "Briefs" column, including Archbishop John Joseph Kain's plans to erect a new Cathedral at Saint Louis, James Cardinal Gibbon's presence in Rome for the Feast of *Corpus Christi* and an announcement of the golden jubilee celebrations at Notre Dame University. One fascinating "Brief" was the report of the ordination of Father John J. Clifford at the Catholic University of America. Clifford would become editor of *The Tidings* in 1907. Viewed from other perspectives, the first issue of the paper could not be isolated from the context of the times. In far-away Rome, nineteen year old Eugenio Pacelli, later to be Pope Pius XII, was bent over his theological tomes at the Gregorian University; fourteen year old Angelo Roncalli, known to history as Pope John XXIII, was preparing to receive tonsure in the seminary at Bergamo and Giovanni Montini, the future Paul VI, was not yet born.

Related to the local scene, Father Thomas J. Conaty was reading galleys of *The Catholic School and Home Magazine*; the youthful John J. Cantwell was a third year divine at Thurles College and nine year old James Francis A. McIntyre was making his way along the sidewalks of New York en route to Public School #70.

Certainly June 29, 1895 was a great day for the Catholics in California's southland. They now had their own newspaper, not a minor accomplishment for a jurisdiction numbering only 50,000 faithful.

Bishop Francis Mora and the Catholic Tidings, 1895-1896

Throughout his many years in California, Bishop Francis Mora exhibited a keen interest in journalistic enterprises. As a youth he had been an enthusiastic reader of the *Diario de Barcelona*, the leading newspaper in Spain, which was established by ancestors of Bishop Thaddeus Amat.

Mora had been influential in convincing Amat to endorse the purchase of *The Monitor* by the Archdiocese of San Francisco in December of 1876. Subsequently, the Bishop of Monterey-Los Angeles used that paper frequently to communicate with Catholics in the southland.

As early as 1890, Mora felt the need for establishing a separate Catholic newspaper for his own diocese. He asked Joseph Mesmer if such a venture were feasible. Mesmer consulted the city's Catholic merchants and, with the enthusiastic endorsement of Edward J. Roberts and Isidore Dockweiler, a stock company was formed. With a meagre investment, the trio launched *The Cause*.

The short and unsuccessful appearance of that paper and The Voice, its equally short-lived successor, greatly disappointed Mora, but did not diminish his feeling that there was both a need and an audience for such a publishing venture. Mora, however, was a realist and that probably explains the dampened enthusiasm he exhibited when approached by Patrick W. Croake, James Connolly and Kate Murphy with plans for yet another Catholic newspaper.

The bishop offered only a verbal endorsement to their proposal, categorically refusing to invest the meager diocesan funds in so shaky an enterprise. Coadjutor Bishop George T. Montgomery was even more skeptical about hopes for a new journal where four or five had failed earlier.

Croake and his companions were adamant in their conviction and they felt that a locally-based newspaper was necessary for spelling out the Catholic cause. And they believed such a program would be supported by the faithful. Armed with little more than a blessing by Mora and Montgomery, the first issue of the *Catholic Tidings* appeared at the newsstands on June 29, 1895, published from a small three-room loft at 258 New High Street.

In the initial copy of the eight page, four column weekly, the founders outlined their purpose: "The field which the *Catholic Tidings* will humbly aim to occupy is a wide fertile one. In territory, it includes the whole of Southern California, and in population more than fifty-thousand Catholics ... In all matters pertaining to the best interest of the nation, state and city, the *Catholic Tidings* will be abreast of the most progressive."

The new publication filled every expectation of its founders and once it was assured of success, Bishop Montgomery, on behalf of Mora, "did all in his power to help it along." After Mora's retirement, in 1896, the editors of the *Catholic Tidings* kept close contact with the prelate and, on numerous occasions, published articles about or letters from the bishop who took up residence in a suburb of Barcelona, Spain. Copies of the newspaper were mailed to Mora and he eagerly anticipated reading the articles appearing in its columns. He once confided to Father Joaquin Adam that his "happiest day in California was the one on which the *Catholic Tidings* first appeared" on his desk.

Newspaper Chronicle, 1895-1915

It was significant that Pope Pius X, during the early years of the *Catholic Tidings*, observed that "in vain you will build new churches, give missions, found schools - all your work, all your efforts will be destroyed if you are not able to wield the defensive and offensive weapon of a loyal and sincere Catholic Press.

Psychologically, the advent of the *The Tidings* was well timed and it was but a brief time before conditions commenced to improve in the Church's relations with non-Catholics. There continued to be opposition to the journal, however. Several lay committees urged the editor to abandon the publication, claiming that "it caused the A.P.A. leaders to be more antagonistic than before." As a gesture to those outside the Church, the editor did agree to drop the word "Catholic" from the masthead on April 17, 1897.

Though he had no financial investment in the paper, Bishop George T. Montgomery "did all in his power to help it along." Together with Croake, the prelate organized a branch of the Catholic Truth Society for the southland.

The lecture program of the new organization received unlimited publicity from *The Tidings* over the early years and by the time of William McKinley's election, "the small and ridiculous figure it [the A.P.A.] cut in the campaign was an eye opener even to the most stupid politicians."

Croake, acting as business manager, went from town to town securing subscriptions and advertising to help finance the journal. Where business people hesitated to support the paper, Croake said "the Irish working girls and men, who had nothing to lose, gave willingly of their meager salaries and rallied to the support of the struggling journal."

For financial reasons, the size of the paper had shrunk to four pages by January of 1897. It was at this time that Bishop George Montgomery underwrote a note for *Catholic Tidings* at a local bank. The paper's editorials were frequently aimed at debunking false accusations about the Church by the American Protective Association. An outstanding example would be the contention that "The Pope recognized the belligerency of the Confederate states and that His Holiness then issued orders to the Catholic soldiers enlisted in the Union armies to desert." Secretary of State Henry Cabot Lodge refuted both claims in a reply to the editor and a copy of that letter appeared in *Catholic Tidings* on June 25, 1896.

By January 1, 1898, the paper was enlarged to its original size with the issuance of the first holiday number, a modest edition of thirty-two pages. A beautiful color autogravure of Bishop Montgomery accompanied that issue.

The circulation doubled with the passage of another year. In January of 1899, Croake made the acquaintance of John J. Bodkin who entered into partnership with him. The format of *The Tidings* remained consistent during the early years, namely a tabloid size with few illustrations. News items reflected the times. Like the secular papers of the time, the editors consistently advocated the principles of Republicanism, but unhesitatingly criticized what they considered to be abuses.

The Tidings remained at the forefront of contemporary issues. In regard to the Spanish-American War, for example, the editor "deprecated the idea of rushing into a conflict if it can be honorably avoided." During those years, the paper was not politically-minded but rather devoted to reporting pertinent matters of Catholic interest. Among those issues were the Friars Controversy, the Boer War and the Pious Fund. The latter case was first mentioned during 1899 when the editor boldly proclaimed that "there is no doubt that the government of Mexico owes the Catholic Church of California a very large amount of money." *The Tidings* reflected a pro-Boer sentiment and carried articles upholding the Boers.

Reading the pages of *The Tidings* during its initial two decades provides a deep insight into the problems and challenges facing the Church locally and nationally during those crucial years.

Bishop George Montgomery and The Tidings, 1896-1902

At the beginning of the 1900s, things had not been favorable to the Church in the Diocese of Monterey-Los Angeles. Catholics, then constituting an unimportant minority in Southern California, were without their own press and not a paper in the city would dare espouse their cause.

Although he recognized the value of the Catholic press, especially in an area deeply infested with the prejudices of the American Protective Association, Bishop George T. Montgomery was skeptical about the possibility of launching a new journal where others had failed financially earlier. Hence, it was that the *Catholic Tidings* was founded almost against the bishop's judgment and advice. Patrick W. Croake later wrote that Montgomery "was quickly won over and once it was started, he did all in his power to help it along."

While Montgomery had neither stock nor capital invested in the concern, its editor noted later, "It may be truly said that during the several years of its struggle, its light would have gone out at any time were his favor withdrawn." Though he made it clear to Croake that the diocese was in no way responsible for the paper's editorial policy, the prelate felt "assured that it will always be your endeavor to conduct the paper for the best interests of the Catholic faith ...."

The cordiality between the bishop and *The Tidings* was echoed in the journal's columns on many occasions. Croake wrote in 1898, "Our good Bishop has always been the earnest, consistent and persistent friend of the paper. In season and out of season, he has advocated its claims and urged upon his priests and people the necessity of supporting their home paper."

There was no question about Montgomery's views on this matter for he noted that "to my mind every dollar spent in support of the Catholic press has two great effects. It is invaluable personally to those rendering the assistance; it is of immense value to the parish where the help is given, through the intelligent and wholesome interest in all things Catholic."

The pages of *The Tidings* were always open to Montgomery. When the National Education Association met in Los Angeles during July of 1899, the paper carried the prelate's address on the religious element in the formation of character. At this time, the paper commended the talk as one filled with "broad-minded liberality and true American patriotism."

Throughout the relatively short period of time that Montgomery remained Bishop of Monterey-Los Angeles, at least one of his homilies, talks or addresses appeared weekly in the columns of *The Tidings*. Montgomery was an immensely popular churchman, even among non-Catholics, and Croake once observed that "many people subscribe to our paper just to read the Bishop's forays into the issues of the day."

Throughout Montgomery's years as coadjutor and ordinary at Los Angeles, *The Tidings* remained a private enterprise, owned first by Patrick Croake and, in later years, by John J. Bodkin. As far as Montgomery was concerned, the journal had adhered to its editor's policy, as stated in 1901: "The Catholic press of today must, according to the Third Plenary Council of Baltimore, be thoroughly Catholic, instructive and edifying, not one that will be, while Catholic in name and pretense, non-Catholic in tone and spirit, disrespectful to constituted authority or biting and uncharitable to Catholic brethren."

Editorship of John J. Bodkin, 1899-1904

Every newspaper is an extension of its editor's genius and *The Tidings* has been no exception. The name of John J. Bodkin was etched deeply onto the masthead of the paper during his five year tenure.

John J. Bodkin, the eleventh of fifteen children, was born at Tuam, County Galway, Ireland, on November 25, 1841. He came to the United States in 1867, and took a teaching position at Saint Genevieve, Missouri. In 1869, he moved to Texas where he taught in "the first Catholic school in the City of Dallas, the school being conducted in the pastoral residence, a small four room cottage." Shortly thereafter, he married Marian O'Brennan in the Cathedral at Saint Louis. It was during his years in Texas that Bodkin edited the *Dallas Free Press*.

Bodkin came to the Golden State in July of 1875, and the next year was followed by his wife and two children, Elizabeth and Thomas. The family first took up residence in San Gabriel. In subsequent years, Bodkin lived and taught in public schools in that city and various parts of Los Angeles County. The next five Bodkin children were born in California.

During his early years on the west coast, Bodkin traveled in the interest of securing subscriptions and advertising for the *California Catholic*. When financial conditions forced that newspaper into bankruptcy, Bodkin resumed his teaching career in the Los Angeles County Public School system.

Early in 1898, the Right Reverend George T. Montgomery, Bishop of Monterey-Los Angeles, asked Bodkin to become associated with *The Tidings*, offering to personally underwrite his investment in the struggling journal. Bodkin complied and by the end of the year had purchased full control of the paper from its founder, Patrick W. Croake. Before the passage of many months, the new editor had enlarged the paper and we are told that the number of its readers was "greater and its influence wider than any other weekly paper published in this section."

There was nothing pretentious about the journal in those years. It was "put to bed" and printed in a small press room in the basement of the Y.M.C.A. at Second and Broadway.

Bodkin was keenly aware that "the support which a newspaper receives determines its quality" and he took considerable care to emphasize that *The Tidings* was not a political sheet nor a partisan organ, for "while the editor has his own political convictions, and pronounced ones at that, he does not consider the columns of *The Tidings* the place to ventilate them." It was Bodkin's opinion that "the chief value of a Catholic paper lies in its treatment of local topics," and he resisted suggestions about enlarging the journal, feeling that "its small size is one of the chief recommendations of *The Tidings*."

Late in 1904, Bishop Thomas J. Conaty purchased the paper as the official Catholic publication for the Diocese of Monterey-Los Angeles. As his final issue drew near, Bodkin remarked with justifiable pride that "there is not a city in the country where Catholics and their religion are more respected or where the entire secular press is more favorably disposed towards our people."

After his retirement from journalism, Bodkin devoted full attention to the religious goods store which he had opened in December of 1899. When death finally claimed the pioneering editor, on January 25, 1918, one of his contemporaries noted: "There have been wiser and abler men in the world than our old-time confrere, John Bodkin, but there have been few more sincere, when embarked on a worthy cause!"

The Tidings Annuals
1898 – onwards

The issuance of annual or special editions, a popular feature of Catholic newspapers throughout the country, began for the Diocese of Monterey-Los Angeles when *The Tidings* published its first "Holiday Number" in January, 1898.

In the years that followed, such publications were eagerly anticipated by the Catholics and others in California's southland. In addition to numerous essays by recognized authorities, the annuals provided excellent opportunities for reviewing the growth and expansion of diocesan facilities. Generally, each issue began with a greeting from the Holy Father, a message from the Bishop and an overview of current events as they impacted the Church.

Most of those special or annual editions of *The Tidings* were released in early December, when advertisements were easier to obtain. The end of the year also provided an ideal occasion for summarizing the work of the Church during the preceding months.

The special or annual editions were highly informative, especially from an historical point of view. Commencing in 1927, there was a series of regional issues outlining the Catholic presence in particular regions of the far-flung diocese.

There were eighteen "annual" numbers of *The Tidings* published between 1902 and 1921, each of them a notable contribution to Catholic journalism and all hailed by other ecclesial newspapers, especially along the eastern seaboard.

Probably the most colorful of the many special editions was the silver anniversary number issued at Christmas time in 1919. Therein, Bishop Cantwell noted that "when *The Tidings* was started twenty-five years ago, there was not a half dozen parish churches in the City of Los Angeles, and today, we have twenty-six parish churches and eighteen parish schools." The prelate felt that "*The Tidings* may well feel proud that it has taken its part in this noble work."

The longest of the special editions, issued for Christmas 1927, contained 176 pages and served as a veritable "directory" of Catholic activities for both the Diocese of Los Angeles-San Diego and the Diocese of Monterey-Fresno.

The scope of subject matter for the special editions was extended in July of 1934 , when *The Tidings* released its first "Educational Review" which highlighted the Catholic school system as it had evolved in Southern California.

In December of 1936, there was a special edition commemorating the erection of an ecclesiastical province at Los Angeles. Archbishop Cantwell proudly told readers that California had become the only state in the Union with two metropolitan districts. That issue contained the statistics that motivated the Holy See to take its unprecedented action.

Six years later, a colorful special edition was published to honor the archbishop on the twenty-fifth anniversary of his episcopal ordination. That issue won wide acclaim for its attractive graphics.

Among the more ambitious of the special editions was that released to commemorate the fiftieth anniversary of *The Tidings* in August of 1945. At that time, *The Tidings* was hailed by the Los Angeles *Times* as "our revered and respected religious cousin."

There were many subsequent special issues, mostly related to such events as episcopal appointments and ordinations, anniversaries of churches and Catholic agencies and the investiture of three ordinaries into the Sacred College of Cardinals.

Of the many accomplishments associated with *The Tidings* over the past hundred years, none excelled the quality and importance of its special and annual editions.

The Tidings Becomes a Diocesan Newspaper - 1904

From his earliest days as residential ordinary for the Diocese of Monterey-Los Angeles, Bishop Conaty was conscious of the pivotal position of the Catholic press. Before coming to Los Angeles, the prelate spoke to the Saint Paul Union in November, 1898, where he advocated "a strengthening of the apostolate of the printed words by which the falsehoods of history may be punctured and the real teachings of true religion made known."

Shortly after his installation, the bishop approached John J. Bodkin, editor of *The Tidings*, with an offer to purchase the seven-year-old newspaper. Such a proposal was acceptable enough to Bodkin who realized that the paper could become "one of the best publications of its kind in the country."

On July 30, 1904, Bodkin called a meeting of prominent Catholic businessmen at Cathedral Hall to consider a plan "to dispose of his newspaper property and organize a stock company for the purpose of enlarging the paper and managing it." Bishop Conaty attended and warmly advocated the acceptance of the proposal, whereupon it was voted unanimously to organize a stock company under the bishop's name. On October 7, 1904, *The Tidings* became the organ of the Diocese of Monterey-Los Angeles, thus entering the second phase of its long and useful service to Catholics of California's southland.

Interestingly, the paper did not immediately advertise itself as the "official diocesan paper," though it carried a cordial endorsement by Bishop Conaty. It was only on the masthead of August 3, 1906 that *The Tidings* first acknowledged being the "official organ of the diocese."

Bishop Conaty urged the faithful to unite in making the newspaper "a worthy messenger of sacred truth to the homes of our people." He then outlined his concept of the paper's role in the southland as one which would "give the Diocese of Monterey-Los Angeles an adequate chronicle of the activities of the church and its people, to provide a journal in which may be indicated Catholic opinion on topics that may be properly considered in that light, to take note of the other events of general importance and interest and, last of all, to establish a public organ which shall make for constant progress towards that highness of educative aim that is the sense of the Church and of the people ...."

A change in the tenor of the weekly publication occurred almost immediately. The format was altered and the number of pages doubled from eight to sixteen. An editorial in the Boston *Republic* reported that "*The Tidings* is the best evidence that we in New England have that the diocese of Los Angeles (sic) has already felt the stimulus of Bishop Conaty's personality." The eastern paper went on to note that under the prelate's direction, *The Tidings* assumed "authority of tone, a sane and poised point of view and literary fineness."

Conaty made it clear that the diocesan newspaper had to fulfill its commitment "to chronicle all the religious events of the diocese and at the same time to bear every week a message of instruction to the people." The prelate's own forceful personality was everywhere obvious, as evidenced by the strongly pro- Irish and pro-Yankee sentiments voiced week after week. Generally, *The Tidings* remained aloof from the controversial areas then occupying such dynamic men as Father Peter C. Yorke of San Francisco.

The editor of the Bay area's Catholic paper took note of the passivity of *The Tidings* by referring to it as "our lady-like contemporary of the South." A man of letters in his own right, Bishop Conaty maintained a keen concern in the welfare of the newspaper. "As the official organ of the diocese, and in its broader scope as a journal of Catholic thought and a chronicle of Catholic activities, it commanded at all times his bountiful interest."

Bishop Thomas J. Conaty and The Tidings, 1903-1915

Shortly after the transfer of Bishop George T. Montgomery to San Francisco in 1902, news reached the southland that the "Rt. Rev. Thomas J. Conaty, rector of the Catholic University of America at Washington had been formally chosen" to head the Diocese of Monterey-Los Angeles.

The appointment was well received, as reflected by an editorial in the Los Angeles *Times* for April 19, 1903: "Few Catholic clergymen in America have broader reputations than Bishop Conaty, who stands as the embodiment of religious zeal and patriotic love."

Conaty was both a charismatic leader and an accomplished educator, and both those qualities were clearly evident in the pages of *The Tidings.* Early on, the Bishop asked an old friend at the Catholic University, Dr. Thomas E. Shields, to write a series of articles touching on such controversial issues as co-education in Catholic schools.

From the time *The Tidings* became the official organ for the Diocese of Monterey- Los Angeles, Bishop Conaty never relaxed his interest in the newspaper. He visited the office almost daily, discussing with the staff many of the challenging matters affecting the diocese. He was always ready and willing to contribute an essay on some topic of current Catholic interest. Several of his many essays were republished as monographs.

During the decade of Conaty's presidency of *The Tidings* Publishing Company (1904-1915), the paper retained a uniform format and style. And while the bishop had no hesitancy in expressing his personal views, he always encouraged the editors to speak for themselves and for the paper.

There was much space, too much according to certain of the local clergy, given to Irish news in Conaty's time. Indeed a journalistic history of Ireland could be written from the pages of *The Tidings* for the period. The Ancient Order of Hibernians, representing some of the most prominent Catholics in the diocese, received more than adequate coverage in the paper.

Conaty spoke often and he spoke well, as evidenced by the 292 homilies, addresses and lectures filed away at the Archival Center for the Archdiocese of Los Angeles. Most of the bishop's utterances were at least summarized in *The Tidings* and many of them reproduced in their entirety. The prelate looked upon the teaching office as a vital part of his ministry and he was anxious that his words reach the widest audience possible. It was fairly common for the local secular press to reprint Conaty's words as they appeared in the pages of *The Tidings*.

In a letter written in July of 1949, Charles C. Conroy said that "when Bishop Conaty bought *The Tidings* in 1904, he had in mind the establishment of a weekly with many of the features of a magazine something like *Harpers* or *Leslie's Weekly*, or *Colliers*, as they were in those days; but devoted to Catholic interests. The paper for years was printed on very good book stock, until the cost, after the first World War, made it necessary to publish it on newspaper stock." Conroy bragged that throughout the decade of his dominance at *The Tidings*, Bishop Conaty "at all times kept his hand on the pulse of the paper, while always giving the editor a free hand."

The bishop's demise in 1915 marked the conclusion of the second stage of development for *The Tidings*. No bishop since has so dominated the paper or taken a greater interest in its welfare.

Campaign for Native Americans, 1904

Of all the campaigns and causes championed over the past century by the editors of *The Tidings*, none is more memorable or characteristic than the one concerning America's native peoples. Though the overall welfare of the Indians interested the nation but little at the turn of the century, *The Tidings* consistently manifested a concern about the problems pertaining to Indian schools and reservations.

In 1904, the Church and members of the Bureau of Catholic Indian Missions sought to have the Browning rule of 1902, which denied Indian parents the right to select a school of their choice for their children, reversed. Bills were introduced into both houses of Congress for a revival of the earlier governmental policy of granting aid to all Indian schools. *The Tidings* wanted the issue "fought out in the Senate, where the amendment providing funds for pupils in sectarian Indian schools was ruled upon."

While *The Tidings* did not advocate a permanent policy of giving aid to religious schools, it did strongly advocate that the policy be continued for two more years until other provisions could be made.

To aid in supporting the Indians in California, Charles Fletcher Lummis had formed the Sequoia League, an organization that did much for the Banning Indian school and other similar educational facilities. *The Tidings* endorsed and recommended that project with weekly articles that described some of the religious ceremonies, school activities and social affairs that were being conducted for the benefit of the Indians.

Bishop Thomas J. Conaty stressed the need of dealing with educational opportunities and problems affecting so many Indians, many of whom were Catholics. Unhappily, as *The Tidings* noted, the Church's efforts along those lines were often misrepresented by impostors.

It was a happy editor who later quoted a letter from President Theodore Roosevelt to the effect that "inasmuch as the legal authority exists to grant the request of the Indians, unquestionably they are entitled by moral right to have their monies used to educate their children at the schools they may choose."

Roosevelt then directed the Department of the Interior to continue the practice of "free choice" unless directed otherwise by the courts. He urged the passage of the Lacey Bill authorizing the allotment of annuities to the Indians in the same way as their land had been handled, a decision later sustained by the Supreme Court.

In 1913, Isidore Dockweiler, a prominent Los Angeles Catholic and a member of *The Tidings* Publishing Company Board, was appointed by President Woodrow Wilson as Commissioner of Indian Affairs. *The Tidings* congratulated Dockweiler on the appointment, noting that it was "a graceful recognition of Mr. Dockweiler's merit as a citizen."

Throughout Bishop Conaty's episcopate in Southern California, *The Tidings* was consistently and vociferously in the corner of native Americans. The Irish-born prelate gave numerous addresses and talks defending and championing the rights of Indians, and a goodly percentage of those utterances appeared in the pages of *The Tidings*.

In an era when few voices were raised in favor of the Indians, *The Tidings* was never silent about matters touching on their welfare. In this issue and numerous others regarding basic human rights, the official Catholic newspaper for the Diocese of Monterey-Los Angeles came down squarely on the side of the angels.

A Trilogy of Editors, 1904-1906

It was part of Bishop Thomas J. Conaty's master plan that John Steven McGroarty would become editor of *The Tidings* as soon as the paper hoisted the flag of the Diocese of Monterey-Los Angeles. The prelate had been greatly impressed by McGroarty's view of the Catholic press which he felt must be "dignified, pure and true, kindly and sweet, but above all, charitable."

When McGroarty declined the editorship, Conaty contacted an old acquaintance on the faculty of the Catholic University of America, Elmer Murphy, and invited him to relocate to Los Angeles and assume the reins of the newspaper.

Murphy, a native of Bellevue, Iowa, was born in 1878. He had learned journalism while working on the editorial staff of the *Chicago American* and shared many of Conaty's views about Catholic education.

While reaffirming that *The Tidings* avoided politics, Murphy and his successors introduced a number of useful innovations to the paper, including that of accepting political ads for various candidates. Murphy's style appealed to readers as is evident from an observation in the Boston *Republic* to the effect that "Mr. Murphy has convictions, but that is the least of his equipment. Almost every one manages to smuggle a conviction into his life somewhere. Mr. Murphy has, in addition, a style of flashing alertness, a body of critical principles and an exacting standard of accomplishments."

Though he served as editor for only a few years, Murphy gained a reputation in the local community as a first class journalist. At the time of his departure, it was noted that Murphy "has written stories for the paper in serial form that have attracted high regard from the discriminating and he has contributed poetry to our columns under a *nom de plume*, that has called forth warm appreciation of the critical."

Following his marriage to the daughter of Maurice Francis Egan, Murphy returned to the east coast where he worked for several newspapers in New York City. From 1923 to 1943, he was in the employ of the United States Chamber of Commerce, writing frequent articles for the National Catholic Welfare News Service. Many of those essays found their way onto the pages of *The Tidings*.

Though it was relatively short, Murphy's tenure at *The Tidings* provided an opportunity for professionalizing the paper's operation. He had a good rapport with the city's secular newspapers and often he was able to use their more sophisticated wire services for gathering news of interest to Catholics. In turn, he frequently wrote for such publications as the Los Angeles *Times*.

Bishop Conaty held Murphy in high esteem and once confided to his nephew that "Elmer Murphy is the great high priest of Catholic journalism." Given the fact that Conaty generally avoided superlatives, such a comment was high praise indeed.

Following Murphy's departure, there were two interim editors of *The Tidings*, Joseph D. Lynch and John F. Byrne, both of whom remained only a few months. Little more is known than their names which appeared on the paper's masthead between March and July, 1906.

John Steven McGroarty and The Tidings, 1903

Though he never served as editor of *The Tidings* (he turned down the position, much to the annoyance of Bishop Thomas J. Conaty) nor ever was a member of the paper's staff, John Steven McGroarty's influence on the southland's Catholic newspaper was felt for over forty years.

Of John Steven McGroarty, it was said that no man has caught the spirit of California from the beginning of the coming of the Spanish *padres* down to the present time and gathered it together into one continuous golden thread such as this great man has done. "His sense of the religious basis of the original settlement of our state not only illumined his writings about that portion of her history, but ran down through his appreciation of modern-day California."

Named Poet Laureate of the Golden State on May 15, 1933, McGroarty later represented his adopted commonwealth in the United States Congress as a representative from the eleventh congressional district. His column in the Los Angeles *Times*, appearing under the title "From the Green Verdugo Hills," was published for over forty years and won for McGroarty a place in almost every home in the southland.

A man of endless talents, the Pennsylvania-born author and poet spent his early years in teaching, journalism, and politics. Although licensed to practice law in Pennsylvania and Montana, McGroarty spent his life in California and it was there he won his fame.

Though he wrote a number of books, both prose and poetry, the name of John Steven McGroarty will best be remembered for his famous Mission Play, a production seen by almost 2,000,000 spectators, most of them non-Catholics, including President Calvin Coolidge and William Butler Yeats, the famous Irish poet.

In addition to his books on California lore, McGroarty served as editor for some years of *The West Coast Magazine* and his contributions to that journal are a valuable part of California's Catholic Heritage. This great pioneer, born just a month after Lincoln's Emancipation Proclamation, went home to God on the eve of his 82nd birthday, August 7, 1944.

It was McGroarty's vision of the Catholic press that kept his influence on the front burner at *The Tidings*. He felt that the Catholic press ranked "first in importance and usefulness." California's poet laureate applied the term "Catholic press" to that weekly newspaper or magazine, countenanced, approved and endorsed by the proper authorities, whose sole aim and purpose is "to labor in the Church's behalf." The one-time Congressman decried the fact that many Catholic journals of his time sought "to ape the methods of the secular press," giving all too little attention to purely Catholic literature.

Such an approach was paradoxical, in McGroarty's view, since Catholic editors had at hand the most priceless treasures to spread before their readers, if only they would use them. McGroarty said that were an editor "to print his journal twice every day for a hundred years, he could not exhaust his vast supply of golden treasure."

McGroarty also felt that "acrimonious controversies with our non-Catholic brethren not only fail to accomplish any good end, but that, on the contrary, they do untold harm." He noted that the only worse thing was "the scandalous manner in which Catholic editors quarrel with one another." His conception of the "ideal Catholic journal" was the weekly or monthly paper or magazine so conducted, edited and managed "that it can enter the Protestant home with the same assurance of polite and friendly welcome that a Catholic gentleman or gentlewoman would receive in that same home."

His long experience at the Los Angeles *Times* convinced McGroarty that journalism should be of such quality as to dispense altogether with the need for apology, excuse or explanation. He said that "the Catholic press must be dignified, it must be pure and true, it must be sweet and kindly, and above all, charitable. The Catholic journal must seek the highest planes, it must live where it can catch the breath of God from the mountain tops of the earth."

McGroarty's ideals were put into practice at *The Tidings* and perhaps that's the reason "the oldest, continuously published Catholic newspaper on the West Coast of America" has lasted so long.

Herman Rodman and The Tidings, 1906-1907

The life of Herman J. Rodman was posthumously characterized by a longtime friend as the classic example of "the eagle caged by circumstance." The son of a wealthy Saint Louis merchant, Herman had been able to attend the United States Navy Academy by virtue of a presidential appointment. He had achieved an enviable academic record at Annapolis by the time of his graduation in 1873.

The prospects of a career in the navy of those days was not encouraging and the young cadet decided to join his father in mercantile pursuits. something that ultimately proved wholly uncongenial. Shortly after the turn of the century, a Japanese naval officer who had known Rodman at Annapolis, offered him a commission in the Imperial Navy. Rodman had just lost his only daughter in death and he was nearing the end of a final illness. Reluctantly, he was forced to decline the position.

When Mr. Rodman's mercantilistic endeavors proved unsuccessful, he turned to journalism and there it was that his innate creative talents reached their fullest potential. According to an article in the *Graphic*, Rodman "was an active newspaper man whose specialties — real estate and commercial work brought him into close personal relations with men of affairs" in all walks of life.

He worked for several Eastern newspaper chains before coming to Southern California as city editor for the Los Angeles *Express*. During his years with that newspaper, Rodman "read and prayed" his way into the Catholic faith. On August 31, 1906, Bishop Thomas J. Conaty, President of *The Tidings* Publishing Company, approached Rodman with a proposal that he join the staff of the diocesan newspaper as editor-in-chief.

Rodman brought to *The Tidings* the experience of a life-time spent as a newspaper man. From the very outset, he infused new life and vigor into the weekly publication, from his editorial offices in the W. H. Hellman Building.

Gradually the paper was enlarged to twenty-four pages. In December, 1907, Rodman was responsible for designing the annual edition of a spectacular issue of eighty-six pages with a format that was to perdure until 1936. The editorship of *The Tidings* was anything but a lucrative position. Yet, like many converts to the faith, Rodman was filled with enthusiasm for the spread of Catholic principles and he felt that in no sphere could he be of greater assistance than as editor of the southland's only Catholic publication.

Throughout his relatively few years as a Catholic, Rodman gave "manly service" in the cause of the Church. He was ranked among the "most prominent and involved" members in the local Knights of Columbus. Unfortunately, Mr. Rodman's association with *The Tidings* lasted less than a year. The veteran journalist died suddenly and unexpectedly on July 26, 1907.

Short though his tenure was, the name of Herman J. Rodman will long be cherished in California annals for the goodness of his life, the sincerity of his purpose, the earnestness of his life work, his unflagging duty to religion, his love of the Church and his country, and his apostolic spirit in the interest of Catholic truth as expressed in the Catholic newspaper. Following Rodman's sudden demise, Bishop Conaty asked Father John J. Clifford (1871-1954) to serve as interim editor, a position he held for about a year.

Alice Stevens and The Tidings – 1908-1913

From its earliest days, *The Tidings* has long been "an equal opportunity employer," as evidenced by the enlightened tenure of a lady editor from July 15, 1908 to October 15, 1913. Born a Methodist, in Sutter County, Alice J. Stevens (1860- 1947) began her journalistic career with the Los Angeles *Times*, where she worked for several years as a real estate editor. She was first associated with *The Tidings* shortly after her conversion to the Catholic faith, as a contributor to the "Women's" page.

In 1906, at the encouragement of Bishop Thomas J. Conaty, Alice inaugurated the "Young People's Column" which ultimately became one of the weekly newspaper's most popular features. Father John J. Clifford, who served briefly as editor of *The Tidings*, following the death of Herman J. Rodman, nominated Miss Stevens as his successor, a candidacy subsequently confirmed by the paper's Board of Directors.

Reared in a literary family, Alice found no difficulty in expressing her personal viewpoint. It was she who started the editorial column, *El Rodeo*, which was to become a hallmark of *The Tidings*.

A profoundly "human" approach characterized Miss Stevens' editorship. She personally interviewed and wrote feature stories on such leading contemporary personalities as Mother Frances Xavier Cabrini, Cardinal John Farley and Father Bernard Vaughan.

In addition to her journalistic expertise on behalf of the Catholic press, Miss Stevens was an accomplished administrator who insisted that *The Tidings* be operated as a sound business venture. Among her many notable contributions was that of moving the editorial quarters to the Higgins Building, at Second and Main Streets, in 1912. Miss Stevens felt that it was expedient and proper to have the newspaper's offices adjacent to those of the diocesan curia, where day- to-day Catholic events could be more easily monitored.

In 1911, Miss Stevens attended the charter gathering of the Catholic Press Association, which she helped to establish as an organization "to promote the educational, literary, news and business interests of the papers concerned and to establish a closer fraternity among Catholic editors of the United States." At that formative meeting, Alice was unanimously chosen as a member and secretary of the directorate.

In the fall of 1913, Alice resigned the editorship to accept what she said was "a woman's higher place in life" as the wife of William Tipton, a leading legal expert on the question of Spanish land titles. Following her husband's death, Alice moved to Pacoima, where she lived until her own demise, in 1947.

Innovator though she was, Alice J. Stevens was basically a very humble lady. She was the first member of her sex to address the Knights of Columbus and the Newman Club and that she did in the masculine-orientated era prior to World War I. At the same time, popular as she was in her role as spokeswoman for the Church, Alice adamantly refused to allow her name to be carried on the newspaper's masthead.

Her five years as the only woman editor of *The Tidings* are remembered as a time of unparalleled gentility in both expression and tone. Or, as one writer noted, "Alice J. Stevens brought a lot of class to Southern California's Catholic newspaper and she did it in a time when class came at a premium."

Charles C. Conroy – 1913-1925

Eulogized as an internationally known scientist, historian and educator, Charles Clifford Conroy was "a man unique in his generation ... one who was versed to an incomparable degree in the fields of theoretical knowledge," yet remaining "untainted by any spirit of mechanism or materialism."

Charles Conroy (1881-1953) was on the faculty of old Saint Vincent's College in Los Angeles when that noble institution forever closed its doors in 1911. Two years later, following his marriage to Agnes T. Hayes, Conroy was named editor of *The Tidings* by Bishop Thomas J. Conaty, a post he held for the next twelve years.

In 1909 he was elected a member of the *Societe Scientifique* and, in 1912, a Fellow of the Royal Astronomical Society of London. Several of his learned articles were published, one on Innocent III and another on the Reformation. His book reviews were always in demand as were his personal observations on local history.

Conroy was a faculty member of Los Angeles College, the minor seminary in the southland, for seven years and from there he went to Loyola University where he became Chairman of the Department of History. He lived in Southern California during the episcopate of five bishops, one of whom ruled the Church for thirty years.

Although history was foremost among Conroy's interests, his accomplishments in the areas of astronomy, meteorology and seismology were widely known. A paper on the 1933 Long Beach earthquake earned him a fellowship in the American Association for the Advancement of Science.

A gentle man as well as a gentleman, Conroy was decidedly outspoken on certain matters as is evident from his many editorials in *The Tidings*. He believed, for instance, that "the Church in this country was in danger of gradual conversion into a mere organ of social welfare, to the detriment of its fundamental object of divine worship." An entertaining speaker of wide repute, Conroy enjoyed telling about the youngster who wrote in his essay on early Church history, "there was widespread movement in the 18th and 19th centuries called Latitude-in-Arianism."

Greatest of Conroy's written works was *The Centennial, 1840-1940*, published to commemorate the establishment of the hierarchy in California. What little was recorded of ecclesiastical activities in Southern California prior to 1960 can be traced to that highly informative book.

It will be forever lamented that Doctor Conroy's death cut short his contemplated history of Catholicism in California, for he had that rare knowledge of the Church that only a personal association with most of the "transitional priests" could give. He knew them all — and they knew him!

His incredible range of knowledge, tremendous patience for detail and an amazingly vivid memory were his qualities as an historian; but it was as a Christian that he excelled in those sublime virtues of simplicity, humility and courage. At home, in rectory, chancery, classroom, newspaper office and even in dusty old archives, Conroy was thought of as a member of everything "Catholic" in California. His life could almost be described as that of a "Churchman," for to him nothing else had any importance.

To tell the story of *The Tidings* without mentioning the dozen year tenure (1913-1925) of Charles Clifford Conroy, would be ingratitude at its height. He was, to quote a close friend, a "peerless Christian gentleman, a man to whom we shall look as a legendary figure by reason of the gifts with which God had endowed him."

Patrick Henry and The Tidings – 1914-onwards

Patrick Henry has long been acknowledged as one of the most colorful personages associated with the Church in Southern California. His influence lives on in the pages of *The Tidings*, where he labored to further the ideals and objectives of the journalistic apostolate.

Born January 29, 1876, in County Sligo, Ireland, Pat worked for a time as a bookkeeper in England. And it was there that he married Carrie Smith on October 1, 1902, a union blessed with five children.

Early in the century, the Henrys moved to Canada. In 1908, Pat became a regular contributor to the *Northwest Review* and, eleven years later, its editor. The Winnipeg newspaper served an area extending from Ontario to the Pacific and from the United States boundary to the north pole. Pat once speculated that he had seven-tenths of a reader for every one hundred square miles of territory.

Shortly after coming to Los Angeles, Mr. Henry founded the *Irish Review*, wherein he expounded his belief that the rights of small nations should be proclaimed "in words of thunder." The newspaper lasted for only thirteen issues.

Pat first became associated with *The Tidings* in 1924, when he joined the staff of the southland's Catholic newspaper as a "stringer." In his earliest days, he travelled the length and breadth of the diocese, gleaning material for special editions.

With his ever-present pipe and never-faltering Celtic humor, the veteran journalist developed an identity with the Catholic reading public unparalleled to that time. His fascinating and unique essays and stories touched practically every phase of the Christian lifestyle.

Pat Henry wore many hats during his career under six editors at *The Tidings*. He wrote a weekly column, "About People", featuring interviews with visiting dignitaries and local personalities. His contributions to "We Hear from Ireland", which appeared under the name Sean O'Rahilly, lent strong support to the movement for the Emerald Isle's independence.

One of Pat's most popular series, published in the fall of 1945, was devoted to his "memories" of earlier days in the City of *Nuestra Senora de los Angeles.* Therein the indomitable journalist chronicled the growth of Catholic life in Southern California as recorded in early issues of *The Tidings.*

During his thirty-five years with the newspaper, Pat saw the circulation increase from 2,500 to 90,000. But all the while, numbers never impressed him so much as quality. To the very end, he wrote his articles and essays in longhand, careful always about detail and accuracy. When this unpretentious and humble man died, in 1959, he was credited by Cardinal James Francis McIntyre with being among the "major architects" of the Catholic "image" for the Church in California's southland.

Through his many years at *The Tidings,* Patrick Henry strove to further the objectives of Catholic journalism. He believed, as did Pope John XXIII after him, that "one of the most effective ways to serve God, to reach into the home, to achieve understanding, is precisely the Catholic press."

Newspaper Chronicle– 1915-1935

During the early years of Bishop Cantwell's tenure in the Diocese of Monterey-Los Angeles, the editors of *The Tidings* differed widely in their opinion as to what a Catholic newspaper should be. Happily, the bishop made little effort to interject his own personal views.

The circulation of *The Tidings* doubled during those years as the paper began advertising itself as "the Catholic voice from Gilroy to the Mexican border." Advertisers increasingly supported *The Tidings*, as is evidenced by one Christmas annual which reached 184 pages.

Father Thomas K. Gorman, the paper's second priest-editor, brought to the paper mature scholarship, clear vision and fine judgment, the result of which were obvious in the editorial pages and elsewhere. No week passed without some technical improvement or the addition of some new feature.

Gorman believed in emphasizing the "news" in the paper, and under his direction, *The Tidings* discarded its old magazine format and devoted more space to local, national and international events. In 1926, a 212 page annual, the largest in its history, was published by *The Tidings* and, in that same year, the paper campaigned successfully for funds with which to build a preparatory seminary for the far-flung diocese.

The largest bound volume to date was published in 1927. Three times that year, the staff of *The Tidings* was forced to move within the Higgins Building. At the close of 1928, the "50,000 Circulation Club" was inaugurated, bringing the number of subscribers to an all-time high. During the late 1920s, Los Angeles once again became a battleground of bigotry when the Ku Klux Klan revived many aspects of the old American Protective Association. The activities of the KKK were cloaked under the pretense of meeting a peculiar local challenge, anti-foreignism. For some unexplained reason, this group included Japanese, Blacks and Catholics.

Patrick Henry, the colorful columnist for *The Tidings*, referred to 1928 as the "fightingist" year ever for the newspaper. Another writer conceded, noting that if Alfred Smith were to win the election for president, he would "have to fight against all the calumnies that have been invented for the last four hundred years to discredit the Catholic Church."

During the first ten weeks of 1930, Msgr. Fulton J. Sheen was given center stage in *The Tidings* with his series of essays on the "New Paganism." In subsequent issues, many of Sheen's talks were repeated.

In February of that same year, *The Tidings* announced the advent the "Catholic Hour" and published the first of Father (later Archbishop) Robert E. Lucey's lectures over radio on the "St. Anthony Hour." That series ran for over two years and was enthusiastically received by the readership

The Tidings published a sesquicentennial edition in 1931, when the establishment of the *Pueblo de Nuestra Senora de los Angeles* was commemorated. That occasion also marked the initial visit to the area of Archbishop Pietro Fumasoni-Biondi, Apostolic Delegate to the United States, who came to offer Mass in the Los Angeles Memorial Coliseum, an event attended by 105,000 people.

In 1933, *The Tidings* was a leading campaigner in another statewide effort to exempt California's private schools from property taxes by constitutional amendment. The earthquake of that same year received wide attention in the paper, which reported the extensive damage done to buildings, forty-two of which were ecclesial structures.

There were all kinds of issues addressed during those years in the pages of *The Tidings*. In Father John Dunne's editorship, for example, the paper publicly sympathized with Emperor Haile Selassie whose speech before the League of Nations "should cause the American nation to bow in shame ... for we have misled Ethiopia into putting faith in American leadership."

Rt. Rev. John J. Cantwell and The Tidings, 1917-1947

Bishop John J. Cantwell continued his predecessor's general policies in regard to *The Tidings*, the "official diocesan organ" and, from the very outset and during the thirty years of his presidency of the paper both as bishop and archbishop, he took no active part in directing its affairs.

At the same time, as President of *The Tidings* Publishing Company, Cantwell can be credited with giving at least his tacit blessings for the overall tenor of the paper's editorial positions.

At Cantwell's behest, *The Tidings* scored the evils of communism as early as 1920, noting that "original documents issued by the Bolsheviki themselves leave no doubt that their purpose was the destruction of Christianity as a concomitant to the overthrow of the economic and social fabric which is the basis of present civilization."

With the increased coverage made possible after the establishment, in 1920, of the N.C.W.C. News Service, *The Tidings* immersed itself in a host of contemporary issues such as women suffrage, immigration, morality of strikes, child labor and Federal control of education.

It is evident that Bishop Cantwell favored the Democratic candidate in the 1932 election. He regarded Franklin D. Roosevelt as "a religious man" who "is one of the few leaders of nations who does not hesitate to invoke the blessings of God and to practice his own episcopal beliefs."

Though he had known Herbert Hoover for some years, the bishop felt that the president "got a memorable defeat. He deserved no better." He attributed Hoover's election, in 1928, "to a wave of bigotry and intolerance which he did nothing to suppress." Hoover had profited, said Cantwell, "by evil things, and now he has paid the penalty."

The prelate's personal views were never publicly disclosed, for obvious reasons, and in response to an accusation that the Church was "swinging to the left," the editor of *The Tidings* responded only that "if the left means that she is on the side of the oppressed, the opinion is profoundly correct."

Neither the bishop nor *The Tidings* commented directly on Detroit's "Radio Priest," Father Charles E. Coughlin, though it did call attention to the fact that he was speaking as a citizen and not for the Catholic Church. Therefore, "his opinions are only as good as his arguments." Cantwell's article on " the Motion Picture Industry" was published by *The Tidings* in the mid 1930s, and that document became the most concrete pronouncement ever made on the subject.

Throughout his thirty years as titular director of *The Tidings*, John J. Cantwell scrupulously avoided any personal involvement in the occasional, but unavoidable altercations that characterize any worthwhile journalistic enterprise.

While expecting the diocesan publication to reflect his own general views, the prelate placed complete confidence in the discretion of his various editors and there is no evidence that he ever found that trust inadequate. That the newspaper prospered under such a policy is obvious from several sources.

A national Catholic magazine observed, in 1942, that *The Tidings* "now indicates that it is possible to produce a lively diocesan paper without confusing Christian militancy with chronic belligerency."

Formation of The NCWC and Its News Agency – 1919

In 1908, Thomas Hart, editor of the *Catholic Telegraph* of Cincinnati, inaugurated the Catholic Press Association "to promote the educational, literary, and business interests of the papers concerned and to establish a closer fraternity among Catholic editors of the United States.

From the very outset, *The Tidings* sought affiliation with this group. In August of 1911, Alice Stevens represented *The Tidings* at a convention of the organization which was held in Columbus, Ohio and, thereafter, her name appeared on the roster as a charter member.

The news association provided current items of Catholic news gathered from European sources. *The Tidings* leaned heavily on this service both in its news columns and its editorials. They gave the paper a totally fresh orientation along with status among its secular counterparts.

During the years when Roman Catholics were still a small and widely-scattered minority in the United States, the country's hierarchy felt the need for an efficient and accurate means of disseminating information to their people on a national basis. Above all, they were concerned about strengthening communications with Rome.

In 1919, Catholic journalism was completely revolutionized with the formation of the National Catholic Welfare Conference News Service, an agency created by the nation's bishops at a meeting held in Washington, D.C. The new agency absorbed and expanded the functions of the earlier Catholic Press Association. As a result, Catholic newspapers throughout the country took on a more alert and versatile outlook. Their editorial columns became more relevant as news of Catholic happenings from all over the world was supplied by weekly mailings.

Prior to 1919, *The Tidings* and other Catholic newspapers concentrated on local news, with most of their columns filled with articles on religious historical and doctrinal topics together with occasional works of Catholic fiction. The paucity of real "news" had always been a difficult challenge for editors.

By March of 1920, the N.C.W.C. News Service was fully operational and James McGrath, the director, was releasing articles to *The Tidings* of world and national interest on a regular basis. The service also began syndicating columns by such widely-recognized writers as Father James M. Gillis, C.S.P., editor of *The Catholic World.*

The establishment of the N.C.W.C. News Service also provided updated and approved texts of encyclical letters and other utterances of the Holy See which earlier had been almost totally unavailable, except perhaps in pastoral letters written by local bishops.

For almost a half century, *The Tidings* daily received a bulky package of materials from the N.C.W.C. News Service which by 1964, had become the largest religious news service in the world.

Since February of 1976, *The Tidings* has received the Catholic News service by wire, teletype and then satellite all of which make *The Tidings* and its sister newspapers in the United States even more relevant and credible in a world of almost instantaneous information.

The N.C.W.C. News Service now called the Catholic News Service, also works in reverse and, since the days of Charles C. Conroy, the editors of *The Tidings* have sent local stories to Washington for distribution to the whole country. *The Tidings* byline has appeared in many Catholic newspapers in the United States over the years.

Rev. Thomas K. Gorman and The Tidings, 1926-1931

One of the elderly priests of this Archdiocese was once heard to say: "That Tom Gorman was one classy priest. He would have enhanced any job, but he brought special prominence to *The Tidings*.

Thomas Kiely Gorman was born on August 30, 1892, the son of John Joseph and Elizabeth Gorman. He acquired his early education at the Academy of the Holy Names in his native Pasadena. At the end of the tenth grade, he entered Pomona High School. His preparation for the ministry was done at Saint Patrick's Seminary in Menlo Park and Saint Mary's Seminary in Baltimore.

After being ordained to the priesthood by Bishop Daniel F. Feehan of Fall River, Father Gorman continued his studies at The Catholic University of America, where he obtained a licentiate in Canon Law. He then returned to California's southland and engaged in pastoral work at Santa Clara Church in Oxnard and Saint Vibiana's Cathedral in Los Angeles.

In 1922, Bishop John J. Cantwell sent the young priest to the University of Louvain. There he completed his studies for a doctorate in history by writing a brilliant thesis about the influence of the United States on the Belgian Revolution of 1789-1790.

Upon his return to Los Angeles, Father Gorman was named editor of *The Tidings*. A staff member observed that "he brought to the newspaper journalistic experience based on sound scholarship, charity and a spirit of Western initiative."

As editor, Father Gorman's "aim was that no week should pass wherein he could not point to some technical improvement or the accession of some new educational feature." In the five years of his tenure with *The Tidings*, Gorman "tilted with bigots, nailed attacks, and dealt with the pressing news stories of an era which encompassed persecution in Mexico, gangsterism at home, Ku Klux Klanism, the Hoover-Smith presidential campaign and steady diocesan growth."

Though he knew little about and cared even less for athletics, Father Gorman is credited with inaugurating the "Sports Page" for *The Tidings*. His idea was that the newspaper should provide something for everyone.

Not surprisingly, Gorman's talents were recognized beyond the confines of the Diocese of Monterey-Los Angeles. Early in 1931, the Holy See detached all the territory within the State of Nevada from the Dioceses of Sacramento and Salt Lake and created a new ecclesiastical jurisdiction at Reno, with Gorman becoming its first Bishop.

Almost immediately, with sustained and amazing energy, like the fence riders of the old West, Gorman ranged his vast, lonely diocese, spurring the labor of the Church, building schools, parishes, stimulating the works of charity and education.

On February 1, 1952, Bishop Gorman was named Coadjutor of Dallas, a diocesan seat to which he succeeded on August 19, 1954. In Texas, the prelate maintained his tireless pace, placing special emphasis on the apostolate of Catholic education. Repeatedly, he called for a strong religious educational program through the school, on the platform and in the pulpit to help restore confidence in God.

Throughout a priesthood spanning half a century in California, Nevada, and Texas, Gorman exhibited deep interest and concern in the development of the Confraternity of Christian Doctrine for Catholic youngsters attending public schools. He had also actively championed the programs for councils of Catholic Men and Women.

In the midst of his many duties, the prelate found time for the intellectual apostolate. He wrote the story of *Seventy-Five Years of Catholic life in Nevada (1935)* and established two diocesan newspapers, the *Nevada Register* and the *Texas Catholic*.

Gorman never forgot California. His annual vacations in Santa Monica became a time for renewing old acquaintances and launching new ones. He wrote a weekly column for the *Texas Catholic* and fairly often his articles were used by his successors at *The Tidings*.

It was this writer's privilege to know Bishop Gorman rather well, especially in the years of his retirement. He once confided that of all his many priestly years, the ones he enjoyed the most were those spent at the helm of *The Tidings*.

El Rodeo Columns Begin – 1928 (1911)

Some of the most fascinating, penetrating and insightful articles published in *The Tidings* since 1911 have appeared under the masthead, *El Rodeo*, the oldest feature still utilized by the newspaper. The column owes its origin to Alice Stevens, editor of *The Tidings*, who inaugurated El Rodeo in the issue of October 6, 1911. Immediately below the masthead of "An Editorial Rodeo" was the following description:

> A rodeo is a round-up on the range, when the branding is done ...
> This is a round-up of editorial ideas from a wide range of thought
> with the proper brand on each stray.

Miss Stevens used the double column spread as a "mix'em-n-gather'em" of materials otherwise unsuitable or too short for a separate story. Included in the proto column was an excerpt from *Ave Maria* magazine which read: "One mistake to be guarded against in the discussion of Feminism, the emancipation of women, Woman Suffrage, and the like topics, by Catholic preachers and writers, is that of identifying their personal opinion with infallible dogmas of the teaching Church. As a matter of historical fact, Catholic women in more than one quarter of the globe do exercise the right (or privilege) of the suffrage; and we have not noticed that by doing so they are incurring excommunication, major or minor."

Then came announcements about a Conservation Congress, a memorial to Christopher Columbus, the arrival of Archbishop Jean Baptiste Pitaval in New York City and a lengthy essay on "the highest ambition of an Irish mother."

The column appeared sporadically in subsequent issues until February 10, 1928, when it was moved to the front page for a series of extensive essays by Father Peter Guilday on American Catholic history. The column later contained many unsigned communications on issues affecting the local Catholic community, even though, as Pat Henry once observed, "reactions from the readers were not always encouraging."

El Rodeo remained on the front page for many decades and numerous colorful commentaries penned by the editors found their way into the Catholic memory banks of California's southland. Msgr. Patrick Roche elevated the tone of *El Rodeo* to a classical level. In his column of June 28, 1966, the editor used the space to hope that *The Tidings* would find its way into "every Catholic home of the Archdiocese."

"One of the basic functions of a Catholic newspaper, the Popes tell us, is to act as a channel of communication which conveys, in their completeness and clarity, the messages of the Holy Father and the Bishops of the nation to mankind.

"The need of such a channel has been amply demonstrated in the past few years with the Vatican Council. The necessity of distinguishing fact from rumor, the urgency of properly weighing essentials against incidentals in the Church's teaching, the requisite of balancing the voice of genuine authority against the voice of transient opinion, were made apparent as the Council opened its deliberations and decisions to the whole world."

After being used sporadically for some years, *El Rodeo* was revived yet another time for the issue of May 18, 1990, when the editor used its column to commemorate Armed Forces Day.

El Rodeo has served *The Tidings* well over many decades and there is ample reason to believe that future editors of the newspaper will find yet other worthy uses for the venerable column.

San Diego Edition of The Tidings – 1930

That Bishop John J. Cantwell exhibited anything but a passive interest in the apostolate of the Catholic press is evident in his concern that the City of San Diego be provided with a recognized diocesan newspaper.

The *Southern Cross* had been established in April of 1912 as a non-official observer of Catholic activities by James H. Dougherty who believed that San Diego needed its own press to interpret the Church's role locally.

The weekly publication held steadfastly to its founder's original purpose of disseminating "accurate Catholic news to the people of San Diego county." In addition, the paper's editor stated that the *Southern Cross* had "never hesitated to incur expense or to face trouble when called upon to do so for the advancement of Catholic interests."

Initially Bishop Cantwell encouraged the paper. On one occasion, he congratulated its editor and noted that the people of San Diego were "very fortunate in having a Catholic paper to give expression to their beliefs, and to break down unreasonable prejudice."

In subsequent years, however, when Dougherty's published views on such delicate matters as birth control failed to reflect the orthodox position Bishop Cantwell expected of a responsible Catholic newspaper, he personally involved himself to the extent of proposing that the Diocese of Los Angeles-San Diego purchase the *Southern Cross* and thereby place it under official auspices.

Cantwell's "handsome offer" was flatly rejected. Indeed, the publisher responded editorially, reaffirming his position that "no Catholic in San Diego believes that we can be served efficiently from 130 miles away, nor does any Catholic expect any more assistance from the outside in the settlement of its own problems than it has got in the past - an assistance which has been practically nil."

The editor pleaded with his readers to allow the *Southern Cross* "to continue the work which it has carried on in this city for more than two decades. Cantwell reacted by establishing a special San Diego edition of *The Tidings* which entered into direct competition with the *Southern Cross* on a weekly basis.

For a host of reasons, the San Diego edition of *The Tidings* was not well received. Father Thomas K. Gorman proposed that Cantwell write a letter to the priests in the deanery, which he did in mid 1930.

"There has been in the past, a great lack of cooperation in the support of the Diocesan paper, known as *The Tidings*. This paper is not the property of the Bishop. It is not any private concern of mine, but belongs to all of the people of the diocese. I hold it in trust for the people of San Diego as I do for the people elsewhere. Dr. Gorman, your own brother in the Priesthood, is the editor of this paper.

"He is making a very great effort to supply the needs of San Diego in an intelligent and high-toned manner. Local papers from time to time have sprung up. They are purely private concerns, and must not be permitted to appeal to our Catholic people in the name of the Church. Complaints come to us not only from San Diego, but from San Bernardino and elsewhere, of propaganda which represents a local paper in San Diego, called *The Southern Cross*, as representing Catholic priests."

The Bishop went on to gently threaten imposing a tax upon the parishes in San Diego for the added cost in issuing *The Tidings* in that area, if the priests failed to encourage support for the publication. That was a tactical mistake which rarely, if ever, has worked with priests in the United States. In response, the priests did nothing.

Despite the obvious economic strain subsequently placed upon the Dougherty enterprise, the appearance of a special edition of *The*

Tidings did not have the envisioned effect and the *Southern Cross* continued as an autonomous newspaper until August 18, 1937, when it became the official publication for the newly created Diocese of San Diego.

It was only a lack of that public trust and doctrinal loyalty which Cantwell predicated of Catholic journalism that prompted the bishop to interfere with the privately owned and operated San Diego newspaper. He seems to have been quite amenable to the existence of such a publication until a breach occurred in the sensitive area of theological integrity. That, he would not tolerate.

Though John J. Cantwell could be classified as a traditional "churchman," with all the qualities that term implies, he was vividly conscious of his own limitations and he rarely injected himself directly in journalistic or any other endeavors where his personal competence was not plainly obvious.

Rev. John Dunne and The Tidings – 1931-1942

During the summer of 1990, this writer interviewed Msgr. John Dunne about his years as editor of *The Tidings*. The following essay is an abbreviated digest of that fascinating interview.

Things were a lot different in 1931 when young Father Dunne, fresh from a three year course in Moral Theology at The Catholic University of America, walked into the cramped offices of *The Tidings* for the first time. The paper was then located on the second floor of a building at 130 East Second Street.

There were only 2-1/2 people on the editorial staff - Patrick Henry, George Andre and Charles Conroy. Old "Doc" Conroy, himself a former editor, "only counted for half because he was also a professor at Loyola College in Westchester."

There was no ticker tape machine in those days. International and national news was delivered from NCWC by post, except for those non-infrequent days when the mailman "fell in" with friends at the local pub. There were two ancient typewriters in the office and they could be heard clanking away from early morning until late evening. Occasionally a friend from *The Times* would drop by to share a juicy ecclesial morsel for local Catholic consumption.

Dunne saved his pennies and was eventually able to purchase a linotype machine along with the other equipment needed for printing the newspaper. From thereon the weekly was produced at its own plant, a factor which saved money and improved efficiency.

Things were vastly different for the Church in those days. The old Diocese of Los Angeles-San Diego stretched from Santa Maria to the Mexican border. There were 284 parishes serving a Catholic population of 292,000. Though the curial offices were just a block away, Bishop John J. Cantwell rarely came to *The Tidings* office, and even less frequently did he use the telephone. "He left us alone," said Dunne, "except when he sent Barney (Msgr. Dolan) over with some official notices."

Dunne recalls only once being called on the episcopal carpet. He had hinted editorially that President Hoover favored certain actions of the Ku Klux Klan. "His Grace was displeased, to say the least." It was a brief scolding which began in this fashion: "Father Dunne, a gentlemanly priest would not have accused the President of the United State of being anti-Catholic. Your little Irish mother would not approve."

Then, just as curtly, the bishop stood up and said: "You may go, Father." As he passed through the office, he heard one of the secretaries whisper: "Go, and sin no more Father"

The Tidings was more magazine than newspaper in the 1930s. There were upwards of a dozen regular columnists and weekly features that came by mail or messenger each week. "First we put the ads in place, then the regular fare and, finally, the news." And, "when there was space left, we flipped a coin as to who would write the fillers."

There were concerned Catholics around the diocese in the 1930s who acted as unpaid stringers, mailing or bringing in local news items. Photographs were mostly amateurish but quite usable. There was no sports section, but there was a great enthusiasm for such literary items as book reviews. Father John Devlin, for example, attended the Philharmonic every week and would often mail in the program along with his observations on a performance.

Pastors and others were good about keeping *The Tidings* informed on activities at the parochial level. Mary Sinclair and Ethel Bossert cranked out whatever official items there were. "We were much more a family in those days," observed Dunne.

While there may have been less journalistic sophistication during the Dunne years, the paper was attractively printed and highly informative. There was no television and little radio, so Catholics appreciated the role of *The Tidings* as the official newspaper for the sprawling diocese.

The energetic Father Dunne served as diocesan spokesman for eleven years until October of 1942, when he received his "Dear John" letter thanking him for his years of editorship. Then, it was on to the pastorate at Saint Teresa's.

Newspaper Chronicle – 1935-1955

The late Msgr. John J. Devlin, one of the clerical "giants" in California's southland, once remarked that "it didn't happen to the Church unless it was reported in the pages of *The Tidings*." With some few exceptions, that observation was quite valid.

The pages of the local Catholic paper were consistently used by the editors to bring to the faithful all matter of pertinent information about the Church's attitude toward social, political and religious matters. Papal encyclicals were often published in their entirety.

Considerable space was allotted to specific topics, for example, to the ratification of the Eighteenth Amendment and the subsequent campaign against the liquor traffic. From its earliest days, *The Tidings* consistently opposed the Anti-Saloon League and the Prohibition parties which were regarded as "schemes to spend the people's money."

The persecution against the Church in Mexico was treated by *The Tidings* more than any other single question in the 1930s, a factor that explains why "priests and people had united under the leadership of Archbishop Cantwell in a continuous effort to bring an era of peace to the suffering Catholics of Mexico." The political aspect of the Mexican question remained at the forefront. One of the editors charged that "In Mexico, it is not whether a man is good enough to be president, but whether he is bad enough. Seemingly, the worst criminal makes the best chief executive of the afflicted republic south of the Rio Grande."

The establishment of the Legion of Decency was a subject of vital concern to all Catholics, especially those in a jurisdiction often mistakenly referred to as "the Archdiocese of Hollywood." *The*

Tidings began the practice - later adopted nationwide - of printing the classifications of motion pictures. *The Tidings* film critic William Mooring said that the one Catholic newspaper in the country listened to by the industry was *The Tidings*.

Nor was the paper silent about communism. *The Tidings* told its readers that "original documents issued by the Bolshevists themselves leave no doubt that their purpose is the destruction of Christianity as a concomitant of the overthrow of the economic and social fabric which is the basis of the present civilization."

During Catholic Press month of 1940, the editor published criticisms sent in by readers to *The Tidings*. Father Dunne eventually got tired of the practice and thundered that since he couldn't satisfy all the letters, he had decided to throw "them all into the wastebasket." A reader wrote in to compliment him for "at least being honest with your readers."

In the field of labor, *The Tidings* consistently upheld the right of workers to organize into free unions, while simultaneously looking upon the sit-down strike as a "development of leftist psychology." The major issue of the period was World War II. Father Dunne stated that "Mr. Roosevelt's efforts to get us (in the war) received support from the silence of the hierarchy who should have known the futility of all wars."

An interesting corollary was *The Tidings'* outspoken view about Japanese people of American birth. The editor criticized the views of the mayor of Los Angeles as being "intemperate, unchristian and undemocratic" when he advocated depriving or impeding their property holdings.

Many other events were amply covered by *The Tidings* during those years, including the appointment of Archbishop J. Francis A. McIntyre (1948) and the creation of a cardinal for the Archdiocese (1953).

Creation of an Archdiocese - 1936

Though mentioned in its regular weekly edition of the paper, the creation of a metropolitan district at Los Angeles was observed more solemnly by *The Tidings* in a special publication issued on December 18, 1936.

In his "greetings" for that artistically-designed issue, the newly-proclaimed Archbishop John J. Cantwell said the honor and distinction belonged not alone to himself, but to the clergy and laity of Los Angeles and San Diego. The establishment of an Archdiocese had been "done for the greater glory of God and the salvation of His children."

In the lead article, Father John Dunne noted that the year 1936 "will stand out as one without parallel in the history of the Church in Southern California. It will record an event which has climaxed a long period of reverses and struggles followed by one of unprecedented growth and expansion."

Dunne astutely remarked that "never before has any event in local Church history aroused greater interest in the public mind or brought such generous recognition from the press as that which brought Los Angeles to the threshold of the Archbishopric." The editor went on to say that "*The Tidings* feels that it can give testimony to an appreciation of the marvelous achievements of our Archbishop in no better way than to publish a brief record of the years of his labors among us."

The sixty-six page special edition was no less than an almanac of Catholic happenings in the 9,508 square mile Archdiocese over the preceding two decades. Statistics of Catholic growth in the area were truly phenomenal. In one section of the issue was a lengthy review of Cantwell's contributions as Ordinary and, by any standards, it was a most impressive chronicle of ecclesial expansion, perhaps unmatched in the nation's annals.

Included also were chronicles of educational growth, Catholic social action, structural progress with churches and schools and welfare activity. One local newspaper described this special edition of *The Tidings* as "giving Los Angeles a premier status among its sister jurisdictions in the United States."

Among the more interesting historical sketches was one written by Joseph Mesmer about "the first bishop to reside in Los Angeles," Thaddeus Amat. Mesmer had known the prelate personally and regarded him as "a most holy, humble man with a kindly disposition, loved and respected by all."

Another significant part of the special edition featured statistics of the Catholic school system in the Archdiocese, with listings of how many youngsters were then attending classes in the four county jurisdiction.

In his closing remarks, the editor pointed out that the commemorative issue endeavored to show that the honor bestowed upon Los Angeles and its Archbishop "have come in the fullness of many accomplishments and that they have been appreciated by many Catholic organizations." In a rare plea for readers to patronize the advertisers who made the special edition possible, Dunne said that "they have a just claim to your patronage, provided you find upon investigation that they can serve you better or just as well as their competitors." The issue of December 18, 1936, with its tinted photogravure of Archbishop John J. Cantwell, surely must be rated among the best ever published by *The Tidings*.

The Centennial published by The Tidings - 1940

If ever you come across *The Centennial* in an antiquarian bookstore, a forgotten attic or a garage sale, purchase it. A copy of that now rare book would be the capstone of your personal library.

Issued in 1940 to commemorate the hundredth anniversary of the establishment of the hierarchy in California, the 200 page book owes its existence to a letter written by Archbishop John J. Cantwell to the Reverend John Dunne, editor of *The Tidings*, on March 23, 1937.

The archbishop had been thinking about the importance "of getting together some valuable data on the history of the Church in this part of California." He suggested that "it would be a splendid record for the present editor of *The Tidings* and a son of royal Cashel to inaugurate and, in the coming year, bring to completion a history of the Church in the Province of Los Angeles." Cantwell even offered to finance the project!

Dunne entrusted the challenge to Dr. Charles C. Conroy, a professor of history at Loyola University and a former editor of *The Tidings*. Dr. Conroy accepted the commission and agreed to complete the work within three years as his contribution to celebrations recalling Pope Gregory XVI's erection of the Diocese of Both Californias.

Though it was a monumental undertaking, Conroy was able to meet the deadline and, on October 4th, 1940, *The Tidings* proudly announced that "The Centennial, a book commemorating the one hundredth anniversary of the hierarchy in California would be ready the following Sunday. The book was dedicated to Cantwell, the "successor to those who have labored from the early days of Garcia Diego y Moreno, first Bishop of the Californias, to spread the

Gospel of Christ."

Its text was introduced by an essay on the "Rich Background of California" by John Steven McGroarty, the state's poet laureate. It was a masterful portrayal in which the "dream" of converting the native Americans and putting the Church on a firm foundation was brought to fruition.

The central part of the book, compiled by Charles Conroy, featured "A Century of Church History on California" and told the story of the former bishops and the parishes of the archdiocese. In the official announcement for the book, a reporter for *The Tidings* said that "seldom if ever, has one century of Church history provided material of such absorbing interest for reproduction in the form of a souvenir publication."

Advertised as "probably the most interesting souvenir of its kind ever published," the book was heralded as "the most permanent contribution to the centennial celebration." A review of the book stated that "Professor Conroy, not only through his profound knowledge of the history of the Church in California, but also through his intimately personal touch with that history, has produced a work of great excellence from the standpoint of the historian as well as a work of gripping human interest in its incidental details."

Copiously illustrated by photographs of 192 churches, the book also contained sections devoted to educational institutions, religious communities and lay and fraternal organizations.

The Centennial was surely the most ambitious and lasting contribution ever made by *The Tidings* Publishing Corporation. Even today, its pages contain information unavailable anywhere else.

Rev. Thomas McCarthy and The Tidings – 1942-1949

In 1942, shortly after receiving a doctorate in psychology at the Catholic University of America, Father Thomas McCarthy (1911-1978) was named editor of *The Tidings* by Archbishop John Cantwell. His facile mind quickly mastered the intricacies of journalism and, before long, the paper was achieving added local distinction and merited national acclaim.

McCarthy opened the pages of *The Tidings* to new columnists and fresh features that appealed to all levels of Catholic readership. He was once quoted as saying that "the essence of journalism is sensation on the wing." A scholar himself, McCarthy enlarged the paper's library and outlined procedures whereby staff members could study as they prepared their stories for publication. Each employee was encouraged to read a book every month. McCarthy's system worked too and, in 1945, a writer in the Los Angeles *Herald Express* said that "in its own specialized field, *The Tidings* has become one of the leading Catholic papers in the nation."

Editorially, the paper kept abreast of the times. Its friendly attitude toward efforts to organize the United Nations, for example, reflected the Archbishop's conviction that only through some sort of universal agency could any real hope for world peace be attained. When the initial meeting took place in 1945, Cantwell told his brother, a San Francisco priest, that "we have all been praying for the success of the Convention in San Francisco, and we hope that notwithstanding the poor beginnings, that the aftermath will be eminently satisfactory."

McCarthy, a man with a high sense of morality, was easily outraged. He fearlessly waged personal feuds with such luminaries as Drew Pearson ("vicious slander and irresponsible smearing") and

Louella Parsons ("cheap, meretricious twaddle") and with any other careless columnist who treaded on the truth.

McCarthy's successor at *The Tidings* said that "it was always his aim to give the paper proper proportion lest it merit Meneken's sophomoric jibe of a "dismal diocesan rag." And so, *The Tidings* became everybody's newspaper, with features for every member of every household, not alone an archdiocesan chronicle, but concerned as well with the momentous issues at home and abroad, in the turbulent years that have now passed.

Msgr. William North went on to observe that McCarthy's pen "surveyed the contemporary scene with courage and conviction. It was slow to wrath except when Christian principles were openly affronted. Hedging was foreign to his resolute and independent mind. And integrity belonged to the essence of his character."

McCarthy early on entrusted the business affairs of the newspaper to Robert S. Labonge, a seasoned journalist who looked after the editorial department and Robert F. Nichols who became business manager. By the time of his retirement from the editorship, one writer said McCarthy had been "our most forceful spokesman" in every arena of public affairs. "And he has been to all a zealous, kindly priest; and to many, a fast and faithful friend."

McCarthy remained at the helm until 1949, when, in the words of *Time* magazine, "the editor of the hard-hitting Los Angeles Catholic weekly, *The Tidings*, and a leader among the younger, liberal element in the Church," was appointed director for the Bureau of Information attached to the National Catholic Welfare Conference in Washington.

That McCarthy's tenure at *The Tidings* was successful is attested to by circulation figures which show that by mid 1949, there were no fewer than 42,495 subscribers to the paper.

The Tidings Publishing Company – 1943

Though it was established primarily for the purpose of issuing a weekly Catholic newspaper, *The Tidings* Publishing Company engaged in several attempts at publishing books and monographs.

Father Thomas McCarthy, one of the paper's more colorful editors, firmly believed that "a diocesan newspaper can and should accept the challenge to become a center of the intellectual life, the focal point in the cultural development of the diocese." Throughout the years of his editorship, *The Tidings* took that challenge seriously.

In 1943, McCarthy asked art critic Clifford J. Laube, a member of the editorial staff for the *New York Times*, to make a selection of poetry that had appeared in *The Tidings* for publication in a separate volume. The first of the trilogy, printed by Benjamin N. Fryer at the San Juan Press, was released in a press run of 500 copies under the title *The Tidings Poets*.

James L. Duff, editor of the volume, who served as coordinator for poetry in *The Tidings*, earnestly hoped that the series would "save from loss and oblivion many a poem that will be read and re-read with joy and appreciation long after the page on which it originally appeared will have become a part of the paper drive." A second volume was published in 1944 and a third in 1945. The latter two books were printed by Grant Dahlstrom at the Castle Press in Pasadena, Only a few copies of the trilogy were actually sold. Most were used as promotional gifts to new subscribers or as Christmas presents from the archbishop. Unhappily, this aspect of publishing was anything but financially rewarding.

It was also in 1945 that *The Tidings* Publishing Company issued in book format a series of fifty-two lectures on the Liturgy by the Reverend Robert E. Brennan. In his Foreword to the 156 page tome, Archbishop John Cantwell said that "the laity will find them written in a language adapted to their way of thinking; the Sisters in schools will find them a model of the mind of the Church; the clergy should welcome a balanced and sane treatment of topics that are close to their hand and heart.

In 1950, *The Tidings* published a booklet, *Holy Year Pilgrimage* containing essays by Msgr. William E. North that had appeared previously in the paper. The fifty-one page monograph reproduced the chronicle of the official tour under the leadership of Archbishop J. Francis A. McIntyre. Harvey Aulbach provided the photographs for the journey which was extended to include France, Spain and Portugal.

Another monograph, this one also printed by Kellow Brown, was issued as a narrative for the *Flight to Rome* for the investiture of the "first cardinal of the far west," Archbishop J. Francis A. McIntyre, in January, 1953. The text of that forty-six page booklet was also written by North, with photographs by James Knudsen.

There were other books, booklets and monographs issued over the years bearing the imprint of *The Tidings* Publishing Company. If those works had anything in common, it was their well-written text and their attractive typography.

Golden Jubilee of
The Tidings – 1945

The fiftieth anniversary of *The Tidings* was observed in grandiose style with the publication of a stunning, four part special edition which deserves to be remembered as possibly the best issue ever published. Certainly it was the most informative. A few copies of the massive edition were sewn into a more sturdy hard-paper binding prepared by Jo Mawn.

In one unsigned essay, obviously written by the Reverend Thomas J. McCarthy, the editor noted that for the previous half century, the columns of *The Tidings* had become "an historical record of the coming of religious orders, the erection of parishes, the building of churches, schools, convents and, at the proper time, seminaries for the education of a native priesthood."

One whole section of the jubilee edition was dedicated to a lengthy and illustrated "story of a Catholic family," one that reflected the strength and growth of the Church in the Archdiocese of Los Angeles. Featured were the nine Kanowskys of Saint Paul's parish, a family that "symbolized the development of the Church in this area."

That section of the edition devoted to the paper's actual jubilee was a thirty-two page glimpse into almost every facet of the paper's activity since 1895. Clearly the most memorable part was "Pat Henry's Memories" which dated back to 1914. There was also an extensive interview with Joseph Scott and Isidore Dockweiler, both of whom were already practicing attorneys in their law offices at Third and Springs streets in 1895. The professional cards of the two pioneers appeared in the proto issue of the paper.

The *El Rodeo* column reproduced Father John Dunne's classic and lengthy essay for Saint Patrick's Day in 1942, concluding with his caustic observation that "the little clique that controls most of our newspapers and all our radio chains would like to give the Irish the works about not handing over their ports" to the Allies in World War II.

Among the several dozen letters from readers, some of whom had been charter subscribers, was one from Mary A. McCormick of Manhattan Beach who said that her family "looked forward to receiving *The Tidings* each week." She went on to bestow the ultimate accolade by saying that she "wished it were a daily."

Though unrelated to the jubilee at hand, there was a most fascinating and extensive essay about the "Progress of the Motion Picture Industry" by William H. Mooring, a *Tidings* writer who was nationally syndicated.

In some respects, the jubilee was upstaged by Archbishop John J. Cantwell whose used the opportunity to announce plans for his new cathedral "that may stand in our fair city to crown the glories of our past and be the immutable witness of our heritage to generations yet to come."

Cantwell outlined the Catholic history of Los Angeles, from pueblo to metropolis, concluding with the observation that a new cathedral "would be a pure offering to the glory of God beyond the mere utility of the moment, a re-affirmation of our Faith in the sight of God and of all people."

The jubilee edition was indeed a memorable publication. A few weeks after its release, a letter arrived at 3241 South Figueroa Street, dispatched from the Vatican. It read: "Holy Father has personally read the anniversary issue of *The Tidings*. He was most pleased and sends his Apostolic Blessings."

The Tidings Directories – Inaugurated 1947

The first Catholic directory issued in California was that compiled by Frederick L. Reardon (1879-1906). That 377 page volume, handsomely bound and profusely illustrated, was released in 1899 from the printing establishment of L. R. Jones in Los Angeles.

In what was the last in his long series of innovative ecclesial accomplishments for California's southland, Archbishop John J. Cantwell asked the editor of *The Tidings*, Reverend Thomas J. McCarthy, to compile a Catholic directory for the Archdiocese of Los Angeles. Though he had been impressed by the directories issued in San Francisco as early as 1938, Cantwell wanted something comparable to those published in the Archdiocese of New York and other eastern jurisdictions.

The first directory, appearing in February of 1947, described itself as "a complete listing of the parishes, pastors and assistants, schools, churches, hospitals and institutions" in the 9508 square mile area comprising the Archdiocese of Los Angeles. Interestingly enough, there were two versions of the proto directory, one with advertisements and the other without. The larger edition numbered 200 pages.

Measuring 8-3/4" x 6", the 1947 directory became the prototype of a series that followed the same format until 1957, when it was enlarged to match the size of directories issued by American Telephone and Telegraph throughout the United States. Though there is no record about the press run of the directories printed over the years, it is known that in 1948, copies were sent to all the subscribers of *The Tidings*.

In addition to a place in many Catholic homes in the southland, the *Los Angeles Catholic Directory* has become a fixture in the intellectual and business community of the area. The Library of Congress has even assigned it a call number.

A glance through the complete set of directories housed at the Archival Center in Mission Hills clearly indicates that of all the American jurisdictions, the Church at Los Angeles has been the most assiduous in recording and keeping track of its personnel, resources and services.

The "covers" for the directories have varied over the years. For the initial two years, there were no depictions and then, in 1951, artistic renditions became popular. The most popular theme has been the Catholic missions (8), followed by Fray Junipero Serra (4) and Saint John's Seminary (3). The number of pages has varied over the years, with 1954 remaining the high mark, with 228 pages.

In addition to page after page of ecclesial statistics, space has been allotted for historical and theological sketches about the Archdiocese of Los Angeles, the California missions, Vatican Council II and a host of other information useful to Catholics. Among the features added in recent years is an alphabetical listing of all deacons and religious men and women.

In the earliest days, several people worked intermittently on the directory, including long-time journalist, John Truxaw. Since 1963, Rose Leman has been referred to throughout the Archdiocese as "the Directory Lady." She is the one who guided the book into the wonderful world of computerology in the years after 1980.

Archbishop J. Francis A. McIntyre and The Tidings – 1948-1970

Succeeding Cantwell as the eighth occupant of the jurisdiction originally established in 1840 under the title of *Ambas Californias* was Coadjutor Archbishop J. Francis A. McIntyre (1886-1979) of New York.

Shortly after his installation, on Saint Joseph's Day in 1948, McIntyre set about to reorganize the archdiocesan curia, to erect a new chancery and to refurbish Saint Vibiana's Cathedral - all of which he deemed necessary to the efficient management of a jurisdiction encompassing an area of 9,508 square miles with a steadily increasing Catholic population.

The new archbishop established secretariats and commissions for vocations, communications, archives, cemeteries and liturgy. He founded the Archbishop's Fund for Charity in 1951, to support otherwise unprovided-for welfare activities.

A building for Catholic charities was erected in 1961 to house the vast network of social agencies actively functioning in the archdiocese. In 1956, McIntyre formally sponsored the foundation of the Lay Mission Helpers Association, the pioneer organization of its kind in the nation.

Among the prelate's most cherished works was the total revamping of the seminary program. He built a new preparatory school in 1954, expanded facilities at Saint John's Major Seminary in 1956 and erected a senior college so as to have a twelve year curriculum equally divided into three four-year self-contained institutions.

Coming from the Empire State, McIntyre thought "big" and nowhere is that more obvious than in his attitude towards *The Tidings* which he envisioned as a west coast counterpart of the New York *Catholic News*. Almost immediately after arriving in Los Angeles, McIntyre launched the first of the annual crusades in which he encouraged the faithful to subscribe to *The Tidings*. While acknowledging that "the *Sunday Visitor* and the *Register* were fine Catholic papers," they do not "hold our esteem as does our own official archdiocesan newspaper."

In all his many letters and directives on the matter, none is more compelling than the one appearing in the October 5, 1951 issue of *The Tidings*, in which he outlined his concept of what the Catholic press was all about. He envisioned the diocesan newspaper as being "the mouthpiece of the Church" for the area it serves. It is the "Town Crier" of happenings affecting the interest of various classes of readers. It conveys information of local, national and international news.

"It gives the opinions of the best minds on current developments in the world and in governments. And this is in the tone of intellectual and cultural presentation. All of this, and more, may be said of your *Tidings*."

McIntyre felt that "the breadth and the scope of the special articles appearing in *The Tidings* have made it a medium of information and of viewpoint beyond the range of news otherwise available." The archbishop always wrote his own letters, something which made his appeals all the more meaningful and compelling. He firmly believed that "a larger subscription list" was essential to the success of archdiocesan plans for the coming years.

Throughout his tenure as the chief shepherd in Los Angeles, McIntyre never backed off in his support for *The Tidings*. In a letter written to pastors on June 27, 1958, he reminded them of "the urgent need of keeping our people alerted and informed" during this critical era. He emphasized "the continuous need of providing our people with the Catholic viewpoint on many pressing issues of the day, and of supplying them with a healthy antidote against the pagan and secular pressures to which they are exposed in their daily life."

Of all the four archbishops of Los Angeles, none was more consistent in this support of *The Tidings* than Cardinal McIntyre. He firmly believed that it was necessary that his people "learn all the Catholic news about what is going on in the world."

Rev. William North and The Tidings – 1949-1957

A newspaper generally reflects the personality of its editor. Surely that was the case with *The Tidings* during the tenure of Father William E. North (1904-1989), one of Southern California's unique and colorful clergymen.

Born in Chicago, young North attended Resurrection parochial school there and old Saint Patrick's conducted by the Christian Brothers. He began his studies for the ministry at Quigley Seminary. Upon completion of his theological courses at Saint Patrick's Seminary in Menlo Park, North was ordained priest by Bishop John J. Cantwell in Saint Vibiana's Cathedral on May 31, 1931.

Five years later, Father North completed his doctoral studies at the Catholic University of America with publication of his monumental study on *Catholic Education in Southern California*, a 227 page dissertation that won wide acclaim in scholarly circles.

North was appointed superintendent of Catholic Schools for the Archdiocese of Los Angeles in 1937 and, a dozen years later, was named editor of *The Tidings*, a position he occupied until 1957. He was honored by the Holy Father in 1950 and 1953.

During his years at *The Tidings*, North built the edifice housing the editorial offices on Ninth Street, tripled the circulation through a cooperative plan with Catholic schools and won national attention and honors for his writings. Under North's gentle but persuasive leadership, new emphasis was placed on local features. Each member of the paper's staff was expected to write one feature story a week and writers learned to use a press camera to illustrate their stories.

There was no dearth of feature material. The archdiocese was in the midst of its greatest era of expansion, with the Catholic population doubling in the post war years. The face of the area was changing. Whole new residential communities replaced the fields and groves that earlier covered the valleys and hillsides of the city and its environs.

To provide new schools, particularly on the secondary level, Archbishop J. Francis A. McIntyre, in 1949, launched a series of Youth Education Fund campaigns. Within two years, seventy-two new schools were built and through successive campaigns, 125 more schools were erected or rehabilitated. And all of that phenomenal activity was weekly chronicled in the pages of *The Tidings*.

North was the co-architect with McIntyre of two successful campaigns to remove taxation from non-profit, private schools via the electoral process. The positive results were all the more remarkable in view of the minimal and reluctant support from the Archdiocese of San Francisco.

North's tenure at *The Tidings* could be best classified as the "golden years." The paper reached its greatest growth, expanding its size and its staff considerably.

The accomplishments at 1530 West Ninth Street were noticed at higher levels of the American Church. In 1951, for example, *The Tidings* won the Gold Medal from the Catholic Press Association for editorials appearing in *El Rodeo*. And, in 1956, *The Tidings* was honored for being the "best Catholic newspaper in the United States."

In an address to the Archdiocesan Council of Catholic Women, North said that "an editor is one of God's abandoned creatures who is doomed if he does and doomed if he doesn't. The word is doomed! The only thing he can safely write about is the weather and the Natural Law, because there is nothing anyone can do about the weather and little anyone knows about the Natural Law."

Holy Year Pilgrimage – 1950

In an address to the Sacred College of Cardinals on June 2, 1948, Pope Pius XII announced that there would be a Holy Year in 1950, the twenty-fifth since 1300 when Pope Boniface initiated the tradition. The jubilee year, the first observed worldwide since 1933, provided a superb opportunity for an archdiocesan pilgrimage to Rome and other areas of religious significance.

In November of 1949, it was suggested to Father William E. North that *The Tidings* take an active part in arranging for the pilgrimage which would be under the personal leadership of Archbishop J. Francis A. McIntyre. A notice appearing in *The Tidings* for February 7, 1950, gave all the details of the official journey and invited any of the "faithful who are interested in accompanying" it to contact the Catholic Travel League.

North arranged to have brochures prepared, noting that the itineraries had been carefully planned for "maximum convenience, comfort and security" on "luxurious transatlantic liners" with reservations at hotels and sightseeing, all at moderate prices. There were to be three tours, two of which would also include Lourdes, Fatima and Saragossa.

The whole scenario was spelled out minutely in the pages of *The Tidings*, where special prayers, listings of indulgences and locations of stational churches were announced. Care was taken that all aspects of the journey were couched within a prayerful context. North was asked to accompany the pilgrimage which sailed from New York City on June 23, 1950, and to act as chronicler for the journey. His articles began appearing in *The Tidings* on July 21 and stretched over the following three weeks.

The narrative of the pilgrimage, written in North's flowing and informative style, was so graphically vivid that the events and sights came alive in print. Among the most memorable happenings mentioned, none was more moving than North's description of meeting the Holy Father.

"He is seventy-four, but lithe and vigorous, moving in unhurrying pace, and when he speaks the room fills with soft music as from another world. You are the last to be individually presented, and then the words he now speaks to all, which you will cherish forever:

"You group around him for a memorable picture. You know he is tormented with work and worry, but he lingers on. The grace of God is in his courtesy. Finally you kneel for his blessing and rise strengthened. He embraces the archbishop. He tells you in farewell of his happiness with your visit. That is all you can remember in the emotion that is yours.

"That afternoon you hail him again, with fifty thousand others, in the public audience at St. Peter's. The pilgrims from Los Angeles have a favored place to the left of the throne before the altar of the confession. You walk with pride as you are escorted to your privileged place."

Upon completion of the journey, the text that appeared in *The Tidings* was revised and then set in type for a booklet printed by the Kellow-Brown Company. Illustrated profusely by photographer Harvey Aulbach, the fifty-one page monograph was offered to those who had accompanied the archbishop's pilgrimage. It is now regarded as a collector's item. The month-long pilgrimage was a tremendous success as is evident from a letter printed in *The Tidings*. Therein Archbishop McIntyre thanked the paper and its readers, noting that the Holy Father had sent his apostolic blessings, "with enthusiastic affection" upon the faithful of Los Angeles.

Los Angeles Receives a Cardinal – 1953

To the day of his death, Msgr. William E. North had a page of the 1952 calendar framed and hanging over his desk. It was the month of November and the 29th was encircled with a red marker.

The appointment of Archbishop J. Francis A. McIntyre to the Sacred College of Cardinals caught everyone in Los Angeles by surprise. While pundits figured that the far west would one day have a Prince of the Church, most thought that the distinction would go to San Francisco, at least the first time.

Communications forty years ago were not very sophisticated and there had been no pre-alerts at *The Tidings* when word flashed out over the wires that the red hat had been bestowed on Los Angeles. Word of the appointment was received by Msgr. North shortly before 3 o'clock in the morning when a friend at Associated Press called him at Saint Mark's rectory in Venice with the news. The actual telegraphic notification from the Secretariate of State came about noon.

By mid-morning, North had arranged a press conference at the Chancery Office. Photographers and reporters from all the metropolitan newspapers as well as newsreel and television cameramen joined *The Tidings* staff at that crowded event.

The cardinal-designate's message to Catholics of Los Angeles was published as the lead item in the archdiocesan newspaper for December 5th: "This issue of *The Tidings* is the official record of last week's momentous happening. The recognition of the Pacific Coast in the Sacred College of Cardinals brings into the focus of the world the deeply religious and American spirit of California."

McIntyre was one of twenty-three appointed to the College. Among the others were Angelo Guiseppe Roncalli (later Pope John

XXIII), Aloysius Stepinac (recently released from jail) and Maurice Feltin (of Paris). One of the new cardinal's first actions was that of appointing Msgr. North to begin preparations for chronicling the trek to Rome where the Archbishop of Los Angeles would be formally admitted to the Sacred College.

Once again, the editor of *The Tidings* measured up to the challenge. His account of that epochal journey, which appeared in *The Tidings* for February 20, was a charming and absorbing narrative of the precedent-shattering event.

The bestowal of the *galero*, conferral of the fisherman's ring, taking possession of the titular church and the reception by various diplomats all were told in a style reminiscent of a playwright. North was especially attentive to one of the well-wishers, a man some believed to be the greatest theologian since Thomas Aquinas: "Someone whispers, 'Garrigou-LaGrange' as an older, whitecowled monk with luminous eyes enters the cortile and you see the famous French Dominican, master of the most abstract treatises in Theology."

Surely the most moving part of the narrative was that telling about the death of Msgr. John J. Cawley, Vicar General, which occurred at Geneva. "For almost half a century, he had dedicated his rich endowment of mind and heart to the service of the Church in Los Angeles. His work was done as in towering glory he beheld the fruition of the dream."

After returning home, North had the text of *The Tidings* articles printed in monograph form under the title *The Flight to Rôme*. When, later, a copy bound in white was given to Pope Pius XII, the Holy Father smiled and said: "Well done."

THE
TIDINGS

Vol. XV.   Los Angeles, December 24, 1909   No. 52

 The Tidings is the Official Paper of the Catholic Diocese of Monterey and Los Angeles. $2.00 per Year

*Patrick Croake was the first editor of the **Catholic Tidings**.*

*Henry Bodkin was the last editor of **The Tidings** before the newspaper was purchased by the Diocese of Monterey-Los Angeles.*

*Dr. Charles Conroy, who served as editor for **The Tidings**, 1913-1925, was also a professor at Loyola University.*

The
Tidings

St. Vibiana's
Cathedral Solemnly
Reopened Last
Sunday

Visit of the Apostolic
Delegate

VOLUME
XXX

NUMBER
6

FEBRUARY 8, 1924

" **F**or the Lord hath built up Sion, and He
shall be seen in His glory." --Psalm CI

Official Organ of the
Diocese of Los Angeles and San Diego
and of the Apostolic Administrator of the Diocese of
Monterey and Fresno

ENTERED AT THE LOS ANGELES POST OFFICE AS SECOND CLASS MATTER
MAY 7TH 1897, UNDER THE ACT OF MARCH 3RD 1879

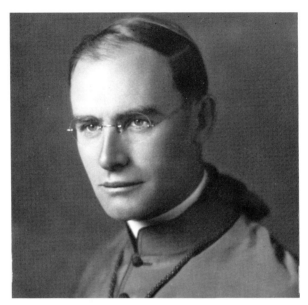

*Father Thomas K. Gorman, editor of **The Tidings** from 1926 until 1931, was later the proto Bishop of Reno.*

*John Steven McGroarty was a great proponent and supporter of **The Tidings** for over forty years.*

The
Tidings

VERITAS VOS LIBERABIT

Silver Jubilee
of
Right Reverend
John J. Cantwell D.D.

1899
1924

Bishop *of* Los Angeles
and San Diego

Catholic Tidings

Vol. I. No. 1   LOS ANGELES, CAL., SATURDAY, JUNE 29, 1895.   PRICE 5 CENTS.

GRAND COUNCIL C. L. A. S.

The Sessions Inaugurated With a Solemn High Mass

The Catholic Ladies' Aid society opened its grand council at its new summer home Santa Maria del Mar, near Santa Cruz, Wednesday morning.

The officers and delegates drove over early to Santa Cruz to attend solemn high mass and received holy communion in a body. Mass was celebrated by Father McNamee, pastor of Santa Cruz; Father Wyman (Paulist) of St. Mary's church, San Francisco, deacon; Father Farrelly, sub-deacon.

The order of business was opened after lunch by Father McNamee, who chose for the subject of his address "The Virtue of Charity." He was followed by Father Wyman, who greatly encouraged the good work being done by this organization, and said: "I hope to see one soon in my parish, relieving the poor and needy and nursing the sick."

Delegates are in attendance from Oakland, San Francisco, Alameda, Stockton, Santa Cruz, San Luis Obispo, Hollister, Santa Rosa and Petaluma.

Mrs. Margaret Deane of San Francisco is presiding officer; Miss Mary Lambert, secretary; Miss Eliza McDonald, assistant secretary. The board of grand directors is represented by Mesdames Paul Lowse, Stella Shahahan, Basilio Laogier, Gonzales and Miss Mary Carr.

ENGLAND'S NEW CATHEDRAL.

The Cornerstone of the Great Edifice to be Laid Today.

The cornerstone of the new cathedral of Westminster, England, will be laid today. The project of the cathedral was decided upon in 1866, and to that end Cardinal Manning purchased a magnificent site between Victoria street and the Vauxhall Bridge road for $275,000.

The cathedral which is to provide sitting room for 8,000 or standing room for 10,000, will be 350 feet long by 170 wide, and inside 100 feet high. Sufficient land will be kept to extend the length 100 feet more if at some future time it should be required. The site not only provides room enough for the cathedral and a lecture hall that will seat 2,000 people, which together with the monastery for the accommodation of thirty Benedictine monks and forty-five lay brethren, it is intended to build, but it is expected to be a source of income, as the ground is now valued at $1,500,000. It is estimated that after the completion of the work enough land will be left to yield sufficient money to form an endowment for the expenses of the cathedral.

The cost of the cathedral will be $1,250,000.

BRIEFS.

Archbishop Kain of St. Louis, Mo., contemplates the erection of a new cathedral.

Archbishop Croke of Cashel, Ireland, will celebrate his silver jubilee on July 18.

Rev. P. Clyne of Carson City, Nev., has been appointed by the governor as chaplain of state institutions.

Cardinal Gibbons presided at the Corpus Christi celebration in Rome. There were a number of prominent Americans present.

A reading circle has been started in San Diego by members of the Young Ladies' Sodality of the Immaculate Conception.

The cemetery chapel of Holy Trinity church, Columbia, Pa., the second of its kind in America, was dedicated on the 3d inst.

June 11, 12 and 13 were devoted to the celebration of the golden jubilee of the Notre Dame university at Notre Dame, Ind.

Thirty-six young ladies received the white veil and entered the noviciate of the Sisterhood of St. Francis at Glen Riddle, Pa., recently.

The cathedral of Carlow has been thoroughly renovated and now ranks among the most beautiful ecclesiastical buildings in Ireland.

On June 5 the students of Mount St. Joseph's college at Baltimore, Md., celebrated the golden jubilee of Brother Alexius, founder of the college.

On June 20 Rev. J. J. Clifford of Monterey was ordained to the priesthood, at the Catholic university, Washington, D.C., by Rt. Rev. J. J. Keane, for this diocese.

Rt. Rev. Rupert Seidenbusch, O. S. B., died at St. Mary's priory, Richmond, Va., on the 3d inst. Apoplexy, superinduced by extreme heat, was the cause of his death.

Rev. E. H. Fitzgerald, D. D., chancellor of the diocese of St. Joseph, Mo., has been appointed assistant director of the bureau of Catholic Indian missions at Washington.

The first colored Catholic church in the south was dedicated at New Orleans last month by Archbishop Janssen. There are 75,000 colored Catholics in the archdiocese of New Orleans.

A bill providing for the commitment of intemperate women to the care of the Sisters of the Good Shepherd for one year, under certain restrictions, has been signed by Governor Morton of New York.

Said Mgr. Satolli at a meeting of the Carroll institute in Washington: "The life and essence of American institutions are in perfect harmony with the sentiments of Leo XIII on the subject of human liberty."

Mother Catharine Carrell, of the Ladies of the Sacred Heart, died June 3 at the Sacred Heart convent at Manhattanville. Mother Carrell was the daughter of John Carrell of Philadelphia and niece of the late Bishop Carrell of Covington, Ky.

RELIGION, LABOR, CAPITAL.

LECTURE BY RIGHT REVEREND BISHOP MONTGOMERY.

Man's Departure from the Law of God the Sole Cause of the Overstrained Relations Between Labor and Capital—Return to That Law the Only Harmonizing Power.

LADIES AND GENTLEMEN—You see by your tickets of admission that the subject I have selected upon which to speak to you this evening is one upon which, in its full import, hinges almost every matter that affects the wellbeing of mankind.

It is evident, then, that it is one that cannot be exhausted in the limits of an evening's lecture. In fact, at first sight it might seem so vast that no man should attempt to treat it all, in a time so limited.

But I shall deal mainly in principles, and principles are short, though the deductions which it is possible to make from them, may be all but endless.

The drift of my remarks shall be towards that great question which is exercising the best efforts of the best men of this age—the harmonising of the strained relations between capital and labor.

I know full well that the questions of capital and labor are sufficient of themselves to tax the ablest and best men of the century, and if I have introduced a third element—that of religion—it is not with a view of still further complicating the difficulties, but to simplify and harmonize them.

I feel in my very heart that if ever the respective rights and duties of labor and capital are to be even properly defined, it must be upon the principles which religion lays down. And still more, if these rights and duties are to be harmonized and if men are to work for the individual and the common good, it must be before that higher court of man's higher nature—the religious and the spiritual.

Therefore I regard any attempt to define these rights and duties and to make men act in practical life for their attainment, separate from that religious and spiritual order, to be time lost and the result to be ever evil, and disappointing.

If this be true, may we not also say that the cause whereby the breach between them seems to be widening rather than otherwise, is due to the fact that that element has not been invoked as it ought to be for their proper adjustment?

The question of labor and capital has ever been a living question. From the time when men first began

to exchange the products of one class of labor for another, or the fruits or products of one section of the country for those of some other, the question has been a living question.

And it will continue to be a living question so long as time lasts, for it enters into the very nature of man as a social being.

We see, therefore, that by nature there is no necessary antagonism between them, and if we believe as is true, that God has given this nature to man, and has established the social order for man's social good, that he must have done so upon lines of perfect harmony—as He has spread about us in animate and inanimate nature—the evidence of the most complete and perfect harmony—in the air, the earth, in the waters upon it, and in the firmament above us.

These earthly and celestial harmonies are preserved because the agents, blind though they be, obey a divine law that marks out their wonderful course.

This antagonism, then, among men, among intelligent beings, in an age when we are so boastful of human achievements, ought to make us humble and more modest in our self-assertion.

I lay it down as a principle that this antagonism comes from man's having departed from the law of God that was intended to harmonise and adjust all man's differences and difficulties, and that the only complete solution to the vexed question is a return to that law.

I lay it down as a second principle that in many of those whose business it is, by their office or profession, by their position of influence or trust, that instead of looking to the general and consequently to the individual welfare they, are actuated by low, mean and selfish purposes, and every attempt to remedy the evil that is not based on God's law and on the crushing of this selfishness, is futile and fraudulent.

And here I shall anticipate the very conclusion I hope to draw from the lecture that that vast army of the laboring masses, who are the victims of this unnatural state of things, stand in their own light when they are cold towards religion or speak disrespectfully of it; whenever they patronise, support or countenance any one of the many agencies at work today to throw discredit upon religion and faith in Jesus Christ, who is their emancipator; I say whenever they do this they are simply riveting more tighter the chains they chafe under.

It is easy to see that under the

Msgr. Benjamin G. Hawkes assists James Francis Cardinal McIntyre in blessing the new building for **The Tidings**, *June 29, 1955.*

Archbishop J. Francis A. McIntyre reviewed stories in 1949 when centennial of California was celebrated in coliseum.

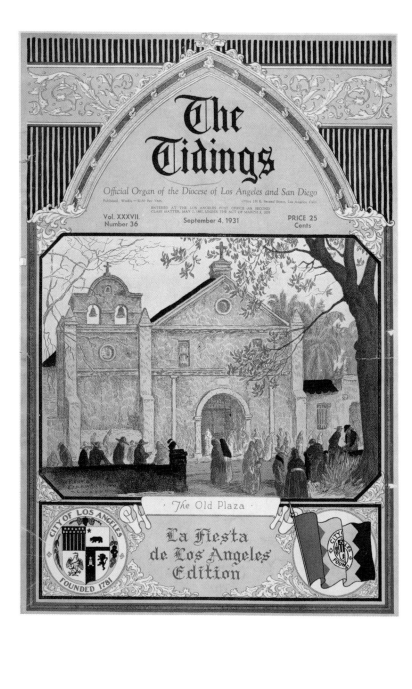

The Tidings

Official Organ of the Diocese of Los Angeles and San Diego

Published Weekly—$2.50 Per Year.   Office 130 E. Second Street, Los Angeles, Calif.

ENTERED AT THE LOS ANGELES POST OFFICE AS SECOND
CLASS MATTER, MAY 2, 1897, UNDER THE ACT OF MARCH 3, 1879

Vol. XXXVII.   September 4, 1931   PRICE 25
Number 36   Cents

· The Old Plaza ·

La Fiesta
de Los Angeles
Edition

CITY OF LOS ANGELES

FOUNDED 1781

During World War II the staff gathered around a small tree to celebrate Christmas. Msgr. Thomas McCarthy is to the left of tree and Francis Labonge, secretary, is seated at left in first row. Through the years **Tidings** *staff has continued to commemorate memorable events.*

Writer Patrick Henry was known as the 'Armchair Philosopher.'

Bob Labonge directed advertising for many years.

THE TIDINGS
OFFICIAL NEWSPAPER OF THE
ARCHDIOCESE OF LOS ANGELES
1895 — 1945

Golden Jubilee Edition

PART ONE

1895   1945

H. KIRBY

***Tidings** office was at 3241 Figueroa Street for seventeen years, 1938-1955.*

*Prior to 1988, the bottom floor of **The Tidings** was devoted to the Borromeo Guild and other offices attached to the chancery office.*

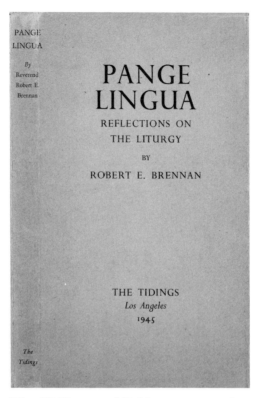

The Tidings publishing company has issued over a dozen books since the 1940s.

CATHOLIC TIDINGS

Official Newspaper of Archdiocese of Los Angeles

3241 SOUTH FIGUEROA STREET

LOS ANGELES 7. CALIFORNIA

Telephone
PRospect 9301

MEMBER
AUDIT
BUREAU
OF
CIRCULATIONS

Msgr. William North holds a staff meeting in the early 1950s with John Truxaw at his right and Charles (Chuck) Johnson to his left. Booklined conference room was used for many archdiocesan functions.

*This view of the editorial offices at **The Tidings** was taken in 1955, shortly after the building was dedicated.*

Before computers, all type was set in 'hot lead' placed in locked forms. Largest issue in handset type was 224 pages in early 1920s. Copy is now set by computer and photo composition.

Tidings In Print For 95 Years

Editors of 'Good News' for 58 Years at **The Tidings**

Fr. John Dunne
1931-1942

Fr. Thomas McCarthy
1942-1949

Msgr. William North
1949-1957

Msgr. Patrick Roche
1957-1973

Alphonse Antczak
1973-1989

1953

CATHOLIC DIRECTORY

Published by

THE TIDINGS

Official Catholic Newspaper

PRospect 9301

3241 So. Figueroa Street   Los Angeles 7, California

The Tidings has published an Archdiocesan Directory annually since 1947.

Cardinal Timothy Manning congratulates top winners in annual subscription campaign. Individuals and schools competed for prizes in yearly drives that greatly increased circulation.

Archbishop Mahony proves he is an avid reader as he scans issue on migrants Mass to inaugurate subscription drive.

*Ted Mullen of Holy Family Parish sells **The Tidings** in 1979.*

*Pressmen hold up issue of 1980 printed at **Daily Breeze** plant in Torrance. Lead story called Vandalism a National Eyesore. Pressman at right wears protective ear coverings to muffle press noise.*

Advertising in The Tidings

Unless it is a totally subsidized publication, the financial backbone of any newspaper is its advertisers. In most cases, the fee paid by subscribers or collected at the newsstand amounts to less than a third of the overall cost involved in preparing and distributing the paper.

There were precious few advertisers in the early issues of the *Catholic Tidings*, especially in the days when the American Protective Association was dominant on the local scene. Even in later times, few merchants felt comfortable advertising in a Catholic newspaper.

The longest and most faithful advertiser in the *Catholic Tidings* and its successor, *The Tidings*, was the jewelry firm of J. G. Donavan (later known as Donavan & Seamans) whose ad appeared in the paper's second issue, on July 6, 1895. "A few suggestions for Christmas gifts" offered by J. G. Donavan & Company in the Christmas issue for 1895 were a sterling silver button hook that cost 50¢ and a sterling thimble which sold for a quarter. Every article was guaranteed "to be pure sterling silver."

James Gordan Donavan, a charter subscriber to the *Catholic Tidings*, opened his first jewelry store in Los Angeles on March 19, 1894, at 167 North Spring Street, where the City Hall now stands. He purposely chose Saint Joseph's day to inaugurate his business.

Both the Irish merchant and the newspaper were attacked by the then powerful American Protective Association, and both thrived on the encounters. A.P.A. handbills called on the public to boycott the Irish Catholic jeweler, a tactic that backfired and actually increased patronage in the little shop at 245 South Spring Street.

Donavan had learned the watchmaking trade in Aurora, Illinois. When the railroad "rate wars" brought down the fares of cross-country travelling, Donavan decided to make a scouting trip to Los Angeles where he saw the makings of a great metropolis. Liking the climate, he returned with enough funds to open his first shop. Donavan became one of the charter members of the Newman Club and his wife was the first president of the Catholic Women's Club. Both sang in the choir at Saint Vibiana's Cathedral.

The family eventually moved to a hilltop above Adams Boulevard, across the street from the famous Holmes ranch, in what became Saint Agnes parish. The Donavans early on became pillars of their parish.

Mr. Donavan liked to recall the day in 1918, when Father Zacheus Maher, the Jesuit dean at Saint Vincent's College, announced to the students that "starting next month, this institution will be Loyola College of Los Angeles." He said that was anything but a popular decision.

By 1975, Donavan & Seamans was the oldest family-owned jewelry firm in Los Angeles. The company had moved five times in downtown Los Angeles and twice on the Miracle Mile, where a second store was opened in 1949.

There have been thousands of advertisers on the pages of *The Tidings* over the past century, but none has equalled the record amassed by the firm owned and operated for so many years by James G. Donavan.

Newspaper Chronicle – 1955-1975

Beyond chronicling the tremendous growth of Catholic parishes, schools, agencies, departments and other assorted ministries, *The Tidings* reported on a host of other happenings in the Archdiocese of Los Angeles between 1955 and 1975, some of which are worth recalling in this context. In every case, the editors consciously endeavored to keep the messenger from taking the credit due the message.

Throughout the 1950s, Catholic high schools began using *The Tidings* as a part of their regular classroom projects in history, civics, English and Religion. In many cases, a full class period was used to read and discuss leading articles as a means of keeping students well informed on current events. Bulk rates were made available to schools taking part in the program, which became one of the most popular ever sponsored by the paper.

Representative Norris Poulson, later Mayor of Los Angeles, inserted a column from *The Tidings* in the *Congressional Record* which expressed the hope that in view of the United States Supreme Court's decision on released time, these programs "will now be improved and expanded so that more children may receive regular training in those moral and spiritual values that will fit them for decent participation in the blessings of a democratic society."

That same year, Congressman E. C. Gathings of Arkansas had a column reproduced in the Congressional Record from *The Tidings* wherein Joseph A. Breig attacked "the shallow reasoning in criticizing a House probe of indecency in radio, TV and magazines."

Of all the many awards and citations that once graced the walls of *The Tidings* building, none was more expressive than the one of June 29, 1955, wherein the California State Legislature extended its official congratulations to *The Tidings* for "significant contributions made in the field of journalism which brings honor and credit to the State of California."

Three years later, *The Tidings* won a national award from the Catholic Press Association for "the best single news story" which was written about the Los Angeles Convention of Protestants and Other Americans United for Separation of Church and State. In that same year, *The Tidings* received a certificate of honor for "the best front page make-up."

During the second week in February of 1959, *The Tidings* introduced a new flag, new body and headline type and a slimmer width in its format. Pages were reduced one inch because paper rolls had been narrowed to conserve newsprint. With those and several other cosmetic changes, the paper's simple, modern typographical style still allowed for an attractive and readable newspaper.

Convocation of the second archdiocesan synod was announced in October of 1959, and formal adoption of decrees took place on December 12, 1960, in Saint Vibiana's Cathedral. At the conclusion of the synod, held on the Feast of Our Lady of Guadalupe, James Francis Cardinal McIntyre was presented with the Golden Rose of Tepeyac by the canons of Mexico's national Shrine of Our Lady of Guadalupe in recognition of his zealous work among the Spanish-speaking inhabitants of California's southland.

The story of those events, published first in *The Tidings*, was circulated nationwide and eventually appeared in over fifty Catholic newspapers. Such national coverage, based on stories in *The Tidings*, became a regular occurrence in later years.

The 1960s were dominated by news from and about Vatican Council II. At *The Tidings*, coverage was provided from several news services, together with copies of the *Council Digest* provided to conciliar fathers and, in turn, passed on by Cardinal McIntyre to the paper.

Circulation for *The Tidings* reached its pinnacle in 1964. In an essay for the *Catholic Press Annual*, John Truxaw reported that "the official publication for the Archdiocese of Los Angeles today has a circulation of more than 125,000 and serves an area with more than eight million population, including 1.5 million Catholics."

The Tidings Building – 1955

When the first issue of the *Catholic Tidings* was published, on June 29, 1895, its offices consisted of two small rooms located on the second floor of a building at 258 New High Street in downtown Los Angeles. That structure was later taken down to make room for the Civic Center complex.

Early in June of 1896, the *Catholic Tidings* moved to the Security Bank Building at Second and Main Streets. With the formation of *The Tidings* Publishing Company under the direction of Bishop Thomas J. Conaty in 1904, the offices for *The Tidings* were moved to the sixth floor of the Hellman Building at Fourth and Main Streets.

Between 1912 and 1929, *The Tidings* moved six times from one suite of offices to another in the historic old Higgins Building, across the street from Saint Vibiana's Cathedral. Then, for five years, *The Tidings* operated out of a building at 130 East Second Street. Between 1934 and 1938, the newspaper was located at 4163 South Broadway. In the years between 1938 and 1955, the paper's address was a remodeled garage at 3241 South Figueroa Street.

In preparation for the paper's diamond jubilee in 1955, James Francis Cardinal McIntyre authorized editor Msgr. William E. North to divert a portion of the assets of *The Tidings* for a new building in a more central location to meet the requirements of a growing, modern newspaper.

Property was acquired on Ninth Street, directly opposite the Chancery Office, and the firm of M. L. Barker and G. Lawrence Ott was engaged to draw up plans for the two story edifice. The modern, reinforced brick and concrete building, built by Ben K. Tanner and Son, contractors, was scheduled for completion by June 29, 1955, the paper's sixtieth anniversary.

The handsome building, envisioned as a long-term investment for *The Tidings* Publishing Company, was designed to include quarters for the Borromeo Guild, Confraternity of Christian Doctrine, Holy Name Society and the Archdiocesan Council of Catholic Women. When finished, the bookstore was the most modern and attractively equipped of its kind in the southland.

The Tidings was housed on the second floor of the building, where ample quarters were provided for editorial, advertising, circulation and business offices. A large basement, with a ramp leading to Grattan Street, contained a mail room, shipping/receiving facilities and a small dining room to serve both the Borromeo Guild and *The Tidings* newspaper. Space was also allocated for storage, air conditioning and parking.

Exactly on schedule, the new edifice was dedicated by James Francis Cardinal McIntyre on Wednesday, June 29, 1955, an occasion solemnized a week later by the issuance of a special edition of *The Tidings*.

For the ensuing thirty years, the building provided rental income which assisted in the publication of *The Tidings*. Even when circulation figures began dwindling, as they did for every Catholic newspaper in the nation, *The Tidings* operated in the black because of investments and income from its building.

Msgr. Patrick Roche and The Tidings – 1957-1973

In 1957, the pastor of Holy Name parish in central Los Angeles, Msgr. Patrick Roche (1912-1982) was named editor of *The Tidings*, the sixth priest to occupy that position since 1895. Born in Lynn, Massachusetts, Patrick graduated from Holy Cross College before entering Saint Mary's Seminary in Baltimore as a clerical candidate for the old Diocese of Los Angeles-San Diego. He was ordained in 1938.

During the earliest years of his ministry, Father Roche worked mostly in educational assignments, both as assistant principal and associate superintendent for Catholic Schools. Like his two sacerdotal predecessors, Roche held a doctorate from the Catholic University of America and that training served him well for the sixteen years he shepherded the grand old lady of the Catholic press.

Admittedly, succeeding North was a tremendous challenge. Yet, there was still a steady flow of local news stories about the continued growth of parishes and schools, development of the seminary system, expansion of the Confraternity of Christian Doctrine and the activities of such organizations as the Lay Mission-Helpers who were sending people from Los Angeles to missionary areas around the world.

It was Msgr. Roche who encouraged this writer to begin "California's Catholic Heritage" in 1962 so that "contemporary peoples could learn about and profit from the accomplishments of their forebears along California's *El Camino Real.*"

Just a few days before his passing, Msgr. Roche gave one last "push" to the apostolate of the Catholic historian: "Keep writing, Frank. People don't remember much about what they hear or see, but they rarely forget what they read. There's something about the written word that touches the soul."

He went on to observe that "Catholics walk taller when they learn about their roots. The honest writing of history is an apostolate that influences the mainspring of the commonwealth." Roche frequently quoted and endorsed John Steven McGroarty's definition of a friend which states that "a friend is one who writes the faults of his brothers and sisters in the sand for the winds to obscure and obliterate and who engraves their virtues on the tablets of love and memory."

Those who read Roche's *El Rodeo* columns between 1957 and 1973 were as impressed by his style as they were by their content. To the very last, the monsignor was a master of phraseology. The record needs to show that Roche departed significantly from his predecessors insofar as he was exceedingly conservative, almost reactionary in many of his views. During his editorship, *The Tidings* lost much of its credibility among those imbued with the so-called "spirit" of Vatican Council II.

Yet, when he retired, he was praised by Timothy Cardinal Manning for his "sensitive and capable management of the paper. *The Tidings* has reflected a true image of the Church and the Archdiocese under your loyal priestly mind and heart."

His Eminence went on to express the hope that "we can all call upon your experience regularly for the continued guidance of the official newspaper of the Archdiocese." And that he did for the following decade.

Popular Columnists – I

Most readers of *The Tidings* have their favorite writers. Over the years, there have been numerous weekly columnists whose essays have "carried" the paper when news was sparse or uninteresting.

Depending on one's point of view, George Kramer was either the best or the worst writer that ever appeared in *The Tidings*. Readers either loved or hated his opinions, but few ignored them.

A native of Kansas, George Kramer attended Saint Mary's College in that state, the Catholic University of America and Marquette University. After serving in the United States Navy during World War I, he taught at Regis College and the University of Detroit. "Doc" Kramer served on the faculty at Loyola University as chair of the History Department and/or Professor of Political Science from 1930 to 1954. Following his retirement, he became a columnist for *The Tidings*, where he remained for sixteen tumultuous years.

Assigned to a prestigious place on page two, his "Headlines and Deadlines" sought to examine and evaluate the philosophy behind the men and events in the news. He always claimed to write "from the perspective of a historian and a Catholic."

Over the years, Kramer's weekly news commentary became increasingly controversial, generating more mail, perhaps, than any other writer before or after. In one news block, the editor told readers that "Democrats think he is a Republican; Republicans think he is a Democrat; Communists think he is impossible."

Few writers could match "Doc's" knowledge of the past. His column entitled "More History to a Mile Along Highways 71 and 79" won several awards and was easily the finest he ever wrote for *The Tidings*.

And then there was Mary Lanigan Healy (1908-1990) whose byline "Among Us" appeared in the columns of *The Tidings* from 1939 until her retirement in 1974. Born at Tucumcari, New Mexico, the daughter of James and Daisy Ann (Brown) Lanigan, Mary studied at local schools prior to entering Saint Theresa College, Winona. Later she earned a masters degree at the University of Southern California and then worked for five years at the Catholic Welfare Bureau.

Mary joined Raymond Healy in holy wedlock at Saint Dominic's Church in Eagle Rock and the nine Healy children were reared and educated in that neighborhood. Later the family lived in Saint Paul (Los Angeles) and Incarnation parishes (Glendale).

Mary Healy joined the staff of *The Tidings* in 1939 and a whole generation of Catholic readers in California's southland came to know her dedication to every facet of parochial and archdiocesan life. She was aptly described as "everybody's mother, sister and friend." A Catholic social function wasn't complete until it was mentioned in "Among Us."

While her column easily became the most popular and widely read feature of *The Tidings*, Mary also wrote for a host of other Catholic and secular publications. Most of the pamphlets emanating from the Confraternity of Christian Doctrine office bore her signature or at least her influence.

In 1947, McMullen Books published Mary's book, *Spots and Wrinkles*, a compilation of her essays for *The Tidings*. A reviewer noted that few parents "have the command over the situation of life, the Christian forbearance or the happy power of expression of a Mrs. Healy." In 1948, Mary won the Family Catholic Action Award which was conferred by the National Catholic Conference on Family Life. She continued an active pace as a popular speaker on the local and national level.

During her final months, Mary was hospitalized. Just a few days before her own demise, she attended the funeral of her eldest son, Tim. To the last, she epitomized the scriptural role of motherhood to her own children and to her twenty grandchildren and three great grandchildren.

Popular Columnists – II

Another popular columnist for *The Tidings* was Thomas Atwill Neal (1907-1983), whose book reviews were keenly anticipated and highly respected by Catholic readers in Southern California. A graduate of Loyola University, Tom entered the book trade in 1925, as an employee of C. C. Parker, the then acknowledged "Dean of American booksellers."

He later hung his shingle at the Hollywood Book Store and, finally, on Saint Valentine's Day in 1933, Tom joined the staff of Dawson's Book Shop, where he became a revered fixture for the next half century.

Probably no other person in the area's history appraised, priced or sold a greater quantity of books. The tiny, penciled code-letters T.A.N. indicated that numerous volumes passed through his hands a half dozen times or more.

Thomas Atwill Neal was a rarity among booksellers in that he read what he sold. Very few scholars (and surely no dealers!) in the southland were better read in the classics. Tom was rightly regarded as a walking concordance. And he was a practitioner of the written word too. One of Tom's most elusive books is the one he wrote about *Saint Vibiana's Los Angeles Cathedral 1876-1950*, of which only fifty copies were printed by William Cheney.

A goodly number of the almost five hundred catalogues issued by Dawson's were compiled (and often illustrated) by T.A.N. Tom also authored six outstanding miniature books, including *Sixth & Figueroa*, his reflections of four decades among the bookstalls.

One day in the late 1930s, San Francisco's Archbishop Edward J. Hanna paid one of his visits to Dawson's. Always enamored by Tom's knowledge of books, the Archbishop suggested that he write a column for *The Tidings*. Not long afterwards, Tom received a deadline schedule from the editor of the Catholic weekly. That marked the beginning of "Books and Backgrounds," wherein Tom attempted "to showcase the facts about some of the forgotten classics."

Just a few weeks before his death at Saint Vincent's Hospital, Tom's autobiography appeared as Volume XIV in the *Los Angeles Miscellany* series. Entitled *Farewell My Book*, it is a delightful portrayal of a well-spent lifetime in Los Angeles.

Tom noted how his appreciation for books had ripened into an intense letterpress love. He pointed out that "the effects of the miracles of Johann Gutenberg are still with us, and are as deep and clear as the impressions of his editions."

If so many of his patrons and friends loved Tom, it was because he lived what he preached, said what he felt and read what he sold. Proud of his faith, he rarely missed daily Mass at Saint Basil's or other neighboring churches. If he was proud of anything, it was that he had a cousin who was a priest (Msgr. William Atwill).

The *liber vitae* or book of life for Tom is impressive. His routine was simple and plain, hardly the kind historians are accustomed to to write about. And yet, there are likely few among his contemporaries who were not spiritually uplifted by having known Thomas Atwill Neal.

One of the longest associations between *The Tidings* and any of its writers was that enjoyed by the late Archbishop Robert J. Dwyer (1908-1976). He wrote a column for the newspaper between 1952 and 1976 and a survey in the fall before his death revealed that he was the paper's best read writer.

Though he possessed a doctorate in history from The Catholic University of America, young Father Dwyer spent most of his priestly life associated with the Catholic press. He was named editor of Utah's *Intermountain Catholic* in 1934 and during those years he not only presided over the affairs of the newspaper, but composed editorials and book reviews, invented a column called "Intermountain

Daybook" and wrote a goodly portion of the local news stories.

After a stint at graduate school in Washington, he returned to Salt Lake City and was restored to the editorship in 1937. He received other appointments but again returned to the paper, by now *The Register*, in 1950. Dwyer's weekly columns were printed in many papers throughout the United States. His literary presence on the pages of the Catholic press during more than 2,100 weeks had a vitality and brightness unparalleled in America's ecclesial annals.

The Archbishop was fond of recalling the words of Pope Leo XIII: "My predecessors chose to bless the swords of the Crusaders: I would prefer to bless the pens of Catholic journalists." Surely those words epitomize the incalculable value of the press as a modern arm of the Church. Dwyer felt that there would always be a place for the priest in the field of Catholic journalism. He noted that "the clergy here is not abdicating its responsibility, but sensibly sharing it."

He pointed out that the Catholic press remains "the standard means of forming an alert and intelligent laity, of raising Catholic literary ideals, and of presenting the Catholic viewpoint in a positive manner, not merely as an antidote for error but as something in itself of infinite worth."

Vatican Council II and The Tidings – 1962-1965

In its issue for December 8, 1958, *The Tidings* announced to readers that Pope John XXIII had convoked an ecumenical council of the Catholic Church, an action done in obedience to what he said was "the spontaneous flowering of an unexpected spring."

For the second time in history, a General Council of the Church had been summoned by a John XXIII. The earlier council had been called in 1414 by the pseudo-Pope, an action subsequently validated when the two other papal claimants endorsed the proposal.

No single topic received more coverage in the pages of *The Tidings* over a longer period of time than did Vatican Council II. At one time or another, all the documents of the council were printed in their totality in the paper. There were also a myriad of background articles and commentaries published about the council, including a lengthy essay by Msgr. Patrick Dignan who surveyed "the greatest timetable that history knows," the Councils of the Church.

From the earliest discussions with Roman officials, James Francis Cardinal McIntyre encouraged the editor of *The Tidings* to pass along "pertinent details" to his subscribers. For example, McIntyre called for a mitigation in the Eucharistic fast, a simplification of the Roman Breviary and alterations in canonical procedure for marriages.

Through the pages of *The Tidings*, McIntyre asked the clergy to explain the purpose and scope of the envisioned council. He requested the editor to draw up a portfolio of relevant historical and theological materials for distribution to Catholics. That McIntyre was enthusiastic about the outcome of Vatican Council II is evident from an interview with the press in which he told the journalists that the gathering "could bring about untold changes: the possibility of world unity, a unity that has got to be spiritual."

On October 7, 1962, McIntyre and Bishop Timothy Manning left Los Angeles for the opening session of the council. Before departing, the Cardinal asked that *The Tidings* call for a "triduum of prayer" for the council's success.

The Tidings reported every facet of the subsequent deliberations with all sorts of interesting statistics about the geographical components of the council, the number of proposed schemes and the results of roll calls.

In his first address, during the Fifth General Congregation, on October 23rd, the cardinal spoke to the 2,363 assembled prelates about the draft of the Constitution on the Sacred Liturgy. While the recording of McIntyre's participation and influence at Vatican Council II must await another time, it must be said here that His Eminence was always open and positive in his reflections about the council. And he encouraged *The Tidings* in all aspects of its coverage of the council.

In one of his personal observations, reported in *The Tidings* for December 14, 1962, the cardinal said that "the Council will stand out in history as a great accomplishment ... We are convinced that this Council will bear much fruit." *The Tidings* was happy to print the results of a national survey published by *America* magazine in June, 1966, which credited the Archdiocese of Los Angeles with being far ahead of other jurisdictions in heeding the suggestions and spirit of the recent ecumenical gathering.

Archbishop Timothy Manning and The Tidings

For well over half a century, the name of Timothy Manning (1909-1989) was an integral part of the ecclesial annals of Southern California. No churchman in the state's history served so long and so prominently at the helm or near the helm of Peter's bark than he who became Archbishop of Los Angeles in 1970.

Few issues of *The Tidings* published between 1946 and 1989 failed to report or reproduce a homily or address given by Bishop (later Archbishop and Cardinal) Timothy Manning. In fact, the relationship stretches back even further because a fair number of Archbishop John J. Cantwell's talks appearing in *The Tidings* were ghost written by Manning who served as the prelate's secretary for eight years.

In addition to pursuing administrative and expansion policies, Archbishop Manning established a priests' senate, an inter-parochial council and a clerical personnel board. He energetically supported a host of ecumenical involvements and warmly endorsed the Cursillo movement. He personally chaired the Commission for Liturgy, established a Spirituality House and erected an Archival Center, to mention but a few of his many activities.

He made a solemn pilgrimage to Mexico City's National Shrine of Our Lady of Guadalupe, where it all began for California, there to thank the Mexican people for their role in bedrocking the faith along the Pacific Slope. It was also in 1971 that the Archbishop was elected proto-president of the newly-created California Catholic Conference.

Throughout his archiepiscopal tenure, Manning was an enthusiastic supporter of *The Tidings* which he often referred to as the 'indispensable mouthpiece" for the Church in Southern California. He expressed a profound disappointment when *The Monitor*, the official Catholic newspaper for the Archdiocese of San Francisco, was closed down, vowing that would never happen in Los Angeles.

Cardinal Manning will be longer remembered for what he said and wrote than for what he did. His God-given charisma shone brightest in the pulpit, on the podium and from the printed page.

Among the cardinal's innovations for *The Tidings* were his annual Lenten and Advent reflections, some of which were re-issued in pamphlet form after their appearance in the newspaper. An examination of the two volumes of his homilies, addresses and talks which were published in book form between 1987 and 1990, together with the smaller selection of his invocations, blessings and dedications, reveal that many of those utterances first appeared in their entirety or in excerpts in *The Tidings*.

In his preface to one of Cardinal Manning's books, Archbishop Pio Laghi observed that while Manning "would never presume to be classified as an entertainer, in so many ways his words, which were always marked by sincerity, solid scholarship and wit, were most appealing and served to draw men and women closer to God through the spiritual enrichment they provided."

Manning wrote many short but penetrating pastoral letters which graced the pages of *The Tidings* and many of them also found their way into brochures and pamphlets. The Archival Center still gets requests for copies of those works.

Surely the most memorable of Cardinal Manning's sermons was the last one he ever delivered, on May 21, 1989, at the Hollywood Bowl. Therein His Eminence of Los Angeles noted that "each member of the Church, each one baptized, has to walk behind the Lord on that journey to the cross, believing, loving, hoping, trusting in His all holy wisdom."

Cardinal Manning allowed his two editors, Msgr. Patrick Roche and Alphonse Antczak, to run the everyday operation of *The Tidings* as they saw fit. They were, after all, "professional journalists" whom he trusted implicitly. But he remained always the "wind beneath their wings" as the presses rolled out the weekly newspaper for the Archdiocese of Los Angeles.

Alphonse Antczak and The Tidings – 1973-1989

If the editorship of *The Tidings* were an elective office, Alphonse Antczak would easily have won the position when it became vacant in 1973. Born on August 3, 1922, to Frank and Adela (Garcia) Antczak, young Alphonse attended Assumption School in the Polish corridor of Detroit, an institution operated by the Felician Sisters.

Al's father, a native of Poznan, Poland, came to the United States via Ellis Island. His mother, displaced from her home in Central Mexico by revolutionary turmoil, walked across the Rio Grande with her parents, brothers and sisters. A cousin is today the town physician in Jesus Maria, their birthplace in Aguascalientes.

The future editor was brought to Los Angeles in 1931, settling in San Antonio de Padua parish in Boyle Heights. His pastor was Msgr. Leroy Callahan who did much work for Archbishop Cantwell in the growing Mexican parishes of the eastside.

After graduation from Loyola High School, Al enrolled as an English major at Loyola University. There he became a protege of the legendary Father Vincent Lloyd- Russell. Al joined the staff of *The Loyolan* and served twice as editor of that college newspaper, before and after World War II.

In 1943, Al enlisted in the United States Army Air Corps, first as an aviation cadet and subsequently as a radio operator. He was on detached service with the Coast Guard for a time to learn airborne LORAN, then a secret navigational system.

Upon his return to Loyola after the war, Al resumed writing for *The Loyolan*. Msgr. Thomas McCarthy, editor of *The Tidings*, was impressed by several of Al's articles about wartime experiences in India and China and offered him a position with the archdiocesan newspaper.

On the Monday after his graduation, Al was assigned to a desk at *The Tidings* which was then located at Jefferson and Figueroa Streets. From January of 1947, the imprint of Alphonse Antczak was felt on no fewer than 2,200 weekly issues of *The Tidings*.

During the ensuing forty-two years, Al witnessed and wrote about myriads of topics touching upon the Archdiocese of Los Angeles, including the five great western migrations - European displaced persons (late 1940s), easterners (1950s), Cuban refugees (1959), Asian boat people (mid 1970s) and the Central Americans (1980s). He moved among these new peoples as friend, advocate and chronicler.

In August of 1973, Al became the fifteenth editor of *The Tidings*. During the next sixteen years, he continued and expanded the policies of California's oldest Catholic newspaper. He served as editor longer than any other person in the paper's ninety-four year history.

During the Antczak years, *The Tidings* operated in the black and continued to help subsidize such projects as the construction of the Education Building, the Catholic Charities headquarters and Santa Marta Hospital. Substantial annual grants were also distributed to numerous inner city parishes during the tenure of the post World War II editors.

During the Antczak years, *The Tidings* won awards for reporting, editorials and layout. Among those citations, none pleased the editor more than the one given for the paper's editorial support of farm workers at Rancho Sespe in Ventura County.

The personages interviewed by Al over the years reads like a *Who's Who*: They include John Kennedy, General Vernon Walters, Philippines President Ramon Magsaysay, King Hussein, Dr. Thomas Dooley, Josef Cardinal Mindszenty, Prime Minister Itzakh Rabin and Karol Cardinal Wojtyla (now Pope John Paul II). Al also served as a Los Angeles correspondent for the Catholic News Service and the US Information Agency. His stories for the latter were published in

Eastern and Western Europe, Latin America, Asia and particularly, Africa.

During those busy years, Al and his wife, Helen, lived quietly in a modest home near San Gabriel Mission. Among their eight PIMA children (Polish-Irish-Mexican-American) is Sister Mary Catherine, director of novices for the Dominican Sisters of Mission San Jose.

During four archbishops, Alphonse Antczak was a primary witness and faithful chronicler for the life of the Church in Southern California. He verbalized his role as that of reporting the works of God's people fulfilling their spiritual destiny.

He was for his generation what Matthew, Mark, Luke and John were for theirs. In scriptural terminology, he has been an evangelist par excellence, an embodiment of the conciliar notion of ecclesial service in California's southland. In 1989, Alphonse Antczak wrote the traditional "30" across his last editorial for *The Tidings*, after a long and distinguished career in the public service of the Church.

Newspaper Chronicle –
1975-1995

Without attempting to enumerate the many issues and news events appearing in *The Tidings* during the period 1975-1995, it might be useful and relevant to sample some of the major outreaches of the paper during those years.

Among the most popular columns was that compiled by Hermine Lees, "Files from *The Tidings*", wherein readers learned about happenings of seventy-five, fifty or twenty-five years earlier. Early in 1976, *The Tidings* surveyed its readership about their expectations of what a Catholic newspaper should provide for its readers. Not surprisingly, the results indicated that most of what it was doing was on target.

Sixty-nine percent of readers wanted local news, sixty percent read national news and fifty-five percent liked the editorial page. Entertainment news, sports, school and women's news were next in order of reader preference.

Columnists were also rated, with Archbishop Robert Dwyer being the most read (56%), followed by Dolores Curran (43%) and "California's Catholic Heritage" in third place (40%). Most people requested more attention to Catholic teaching and the viewpoint of the Church on current events. That *The Tidings* continued being highly regarded by the Catholic Press Association was confirmed by the steady awarding of citations given to the paper during the 1970s.

One of the biggest stories during the decade was the creation of the Diocese of Orange, on June 18, 1976. Officials at *The Tidings* were elated when most of the subscribers in the new jurisdiction opted to continue their subscriptions to *The Tidings*, even after the establishment of the *Diocese of Orange Bulletin*.

In August of 1978, editor Alphonse Antczak summarized some of the programs underway, noting that *The Tidings* had already that year published eight tabloids related to various ministries. He pointed out that stories receiving priority coverage were those dealing with civil rights, the Church in Latin America, abortion, school support and the relationship of teenagers and young adults with the Church. In every case, this same mix was being featured by the secular press, but without any relationship to morality or religion.

After several years of study, Timothy Cardinal Manning announced, in September of 1977, a Retirement Plan for the staff of *The Tidings*. His Eminence noted that he and others had long been concerned for the financial security of workers in their retirement years. The parameters of the precedent-breaking plan were spelled out in a brochure distributed to employees.

In recognition of its support of ecological measures, the editor of *The Tidings* directed, in 1985, that the paper used for the weekly edition be recycled from pulp processed by Golden State Newsprint of Pomona. No news story was reported with greater satisfaction and joy than the one announcing the beatification of Fray Junipero Serra, which took place on the front steps of Saint Peter's Basilica, September 25, 1988.

The internal structure of *The Tidings* Publishing Corporation was altered slightly in May of 1990, with the appointment of a "publisher" in the person of Roy Boody. He was to oversee the entire operation of the corporation, thus allowing the editor to devote full time to the paper.

Alphonse Antczak was succeeded in the editorship by William Rivera, the archdiocesan Director of Public Affairs, who served from October 1, 1989 to May 11, 1990. Msgr. Francis J. Weber then acted as interim editor until Alfred Doblin came aboard in the fall of 1990. He was replaced two years later by Tod Tamberg.

Archbishop Roger Mahony and The Tidings – 1986-onwards

Born and raised in North Hollywood, ordained priest for the Diocese of Monterey- Fresno and trained in leadership as auxiliary and residential bishop in Central California, Roger Mahony had served the Church in many roles - as director of Catholic Charities, pastor of a Cathedral, teacher at Fresno State College and chancellor of a busy diocese before returning to Los Angeles as Metropolitan Archbishop in 1985.

Of all the four prelates who have served as Chief Shepherds for the Archdiocese of Los Angeles, none has been more effective with the media than Roger Cardinal Mahony. No churchman in the United States has enjoyed a "greater press" than the archbishop and surely none is more at ease with the throngs of reporters and interviewers than the one who spiritually presides over the communication capital of the world.

Not only a news-maker in his own right, Mahony has a deep understanding of journalism and its potential for good and bad, both within and without the Catholic Church. As one observer noted after Mahony's first interview with the *Los Angeles Times*: "The archbishop landed in Southern California on his feet and that augurs for a happy rapport with the press in the years to come." Surely, in retrospect, that observation became a prophecy.

The relationship of Archbishop Roger Mahony with *The Tidings* dates from the issue of October 18, 1946, when the paper carried a picture of ten year old Roger and his twin brother, Louis.

As a student at Saint Charles School, Mahony was among the many students in North Hollywood who participated in the annual subscription drives spearheaded in the parish by the late Msgr. Harry Meade. From his earliest years, he recalled that *The Tidings* was a weekly visitor to the Mahony residence.

Since his installation as archbishop, Mahony has been an avid and consistent supporter of *The Tidings* which he described as our "family newspaper" and in which Catholics keep "in touch with one another, with the Holy Father, the bishops and the whole Church." In several pastoral exhortations, Archbishop and later Cardinal Mahony urged Catholics "to subscribe to *The Tidings* as a newspaper that incorporates you into the life of our local Church, that will inform you and form you according to the norms of the Church."

Working closely with the board members of *The Tidings* Publishing Corporation, the Archbishop encouraged the modernization of the paper, along with the formation of an editorial policy board. In its issue of July 12, 1991, editor Alfred Doblin announced to readers that "the grande dame of Catholic journalism had undergone a face lift, a tummy tuck and a little liposuction." Issued once again as a tabloid, the paper would be sleeker, utilizing all the best elements of the graphic arts. Doblin said that within a few months, the entire production of the paper would be executed by "our in-house system." Central objective of The "new *Tidings*" would be to challenge and inform its readers. "Being a Catholic doesn't mean being stuffy. Being a Catholic means embracing all the glorious foibles of the human condition."

The Catholic press can and should be a vital link between the teachings of the Church and the lived experience of that Church. *The Tidings* measures up to that challenge as it closes out its first century of service to the Catholics of California's southland.

The Papal Visit – 1987

Of all the tasks entrusted to *The Tidings* during the first century of its existence, none was more challenging than that of preparing for and covering the visit of Pope John Paul II to Los Angeles in September of 1987.

The journey of the Holy Father culminated and fulfilled a relationship inaugurated in 1774, in the person of Pope Clement XIV (1769-1774). It was he who issued a special indult whereby Fray Junipero Serra was authorized to confer the Sacrament of Confirmation in the missionary foundations along *El Camino Real*.

That link with the past was solidified when Archbishop Roger Mahony presented the Pontiff with a *Biblical Concordance* that had been given to Serra when he left the *convento* of San Bernardino for the New World in 1749.

The major portion of a year was spent in getting ready for what proved to be the most meaningful and spiritual event in the history of the archdiocese. In all those preparations, special deference was given to the archdiocesan paper which was to be the "memory" of the first papal visit to California.

Reporters dug out of *The Tidings* morgue an interview conducted by Alphonse Antczak with Karol Cardinal Wojtyla when he visited Los Angeles on August 29, 1976. There was also a description of the Cardinal's tour of Forest Lawn Memorial Park.

That the Holy Father was cognizant of the place of Catholic newspapers on the local and national scene was evident from a remark he made to *The Tidings* writer, R. W. Dellinger, at LAX: "You of the press are very important."

The Holy Father set the spiritual tone of his visit in remarks delivered at Saint Vibiana's Cathedral: "As the successor of Peter, I come to you today in the name of Jesus. It cannot be otherwise; since every true minister of the Gospel preaches not himself or any message of human origin, but he preaches Jesus Christ as Lord."

Three issues of *The Tidings*, those of September 11, 18 and 25 were devoted almost exclusively to coverage of the papal visit. The moving talk given by the Pontiff at the cathedral led off the issue of the 18th. In his address to the National Conference of Catholic Bishops at Mission Hills, he said that it was a "grave error" to think that a Catholic's dissent from Church teachings "poses no obstacle to the reception of the sacraments."

During his visit to Immaculate Conception elementary school with Nancy Reagan, the Pope exhorted young people to learn "the difference between good and bad influences, and how important it is to avoid those things, such as the use of drugs." The Holy Father met with Buddhists, Hindus, Moslems and Jews, encouraging interfaith dialogue and urging the world religions to greater efforts for peace. Then, at a liturgy at Dodger Stadium, the Holy Father consecrated the United States to Mary and praised the country's bishops for their efforts on behalf of illegal aliens.

Of all the Holy Father's addresses and talks reproduced in the pages of *The Tidings*, none was more touching than the twenty minute homily delivered before 103,000 people in the Los Angeles Memorial Coliseum in which he called upon his listeners "to model their lives after the Good Samaritan whose decision to stop and care was prompted by compassion."

By the time of the Holy Father's departure, Antczak and his staff at *The Tidings* were physically exhausted but spiritually renewed, for in the words of Archbishop Mahony, "He came and walked among us, and we are all gifted and graced for that visit."

Vida Nueva launched by The Tidings Publishing Company

There is a long and rich historical precedent for *Vida Nueva*, the Spanish language newspaper inaugurated on April 10, 1991 by *The Tidings* Corporation for the Archdiocese of Los Angeles.

Catholic journalistic influences stretch back to August of 1846, when the *Californian*, the first newspaper published in the state, was printed on a machine "found in the cloisters of one of the missions." Since that time, the Catholic press has consistently been an active force in California life. As early as 1850, the New York *Freeman's Journal and Catholic Register* carried a regular column from a Sacramento correspondent signed only as "Philos," probably the pen name for Dr. Gregory Phelan.

The first Catholic weekly newspaper published on the Pacific Coast originated at San Francisco under the auspices of Father Hugh Gallagher. *The Catholic Standard*, launched on May 6, 1854, advertised itself as "an organ of the Catholic Church."

Apart from the long list of English-speaking newspapers sponsored by the Church or issued "under Catholic auspices," *La Cronica* has the distinction of being the first published in California for the Hispanic community. Edited by E. F. Teodoli, *La Cronica* was described by a writer in the Los Angeles *Star* as "a substantial paper, published semi-weekly."

La Cronica appeared fairly consistently between 1872 and 1892. When the newspaper got into financial straits and ceased publication, it was succeeded by another Hispanic weekly known as *Las dos Republicas*.

A Portuguese newspaper was distributed in the Bay area under the masthead of O *Vox Portuguesa* between 1884 and 1888 by Antonio Vicente. A second paper, begun in 1884 under the title O *Progresso Californiense*, limped along for five years and was then made over to *Unaio Portuguesa* by Manuel Trigueiro.

Der Californischen Volksfreund was a Catholic paper printed in the German language in San Francisco. Begun in 1885 by Carl Doeing and Frank Diepenbrock, the publication lasted until 1906.

O Amigos do Catolicos originated at Irvington in 1888. The Portuguese publication was inaugurated by Fathers Manuel Francisco Fernandez and Jose Francisco Tavares. After a year, the paper passed under lay control and moved to Pleasanton.

From 1892 to 1896, it was printed at Hayward. The name was changed to *O Arauto* in 1896 and until 1917 it was published at Irvington under the editorship of Messrs. Lemos and Quaresma. In the latter year, Pedro L. C. Silveira purchased the paper and merged it with his *0 Jornal de Noticias*.

L'Imparziale was first published from San Francisco in 1891 by Joseph Morgana. The paper was inactive for some years but was revived between 1897 and 1909 as the *Impartial Californien* under the direction of P. S. Bergerot. In 1901, the Saint Louis *Review* called it "the only Italian Catholic paper in the United States."

Luigi Muzio edited a newspaper known as *La Verita* at San Francisco between 1893 and 1894. The venture started and finished as an Italian Catholic publication. "Devoted to the instruction in Catholic truth and doctrine" of the Spanish speaking people in Southern California was *La Actualidad*, printed from 1895 at San Bernardino under the direction of Father Juan Caballeria. The eight page weekly ceased publication about 1902. In 1897, Constantino Soares originated *O Reporter* at Oakland. From 1910 to 1914, the weekly was owned and issued by the Reverend Jose Silva.

L'Unione was established some time prior to 1922. In that year, the "Catholic Italian paper" was merged with the *Tribuna*. Its name reverted to *L'Unione* when the publication became the official Italian organ for the Archdiocese of San Francisco. It was affiliated with the Italian Catholic Federation in 1931 and, since 1944, has been issued as the *Boletino*. The Claretians during the 1930s and 1940s published a magazine in Spanish called *La Esperanza*, which was available at Mexican-American parishes.

La Luz started in 1949 as the Spanish language paper for the Diocese of Monterey-Fresno. Its name was changed to *Excelsior* in 1950. After 1961, it was jointly issued with the *Central California Register* and finally discontinued for lack of public support.

The most recent Spanish language Catholic newspaper in California and one still being issued, is *Heraldo Catolico*. Sponsored by the Diocese of Sacramento, it is circulated throughout the state.

Vida Nueva then has a noble Catholic and Hispanic lineage in the Golden State. From all initial reports, it has been favorably received and very well might revolutionize the whole concept of Catholic journalism in the United States.

A Look Forward

Historians are notoriously poor prophets and there is no reason to think that this writer has any special insight about the future of *The Tidings*. But, what is past is prologue and, if the accomplishments of *The Tidings* over the years are any indication, there is bright future for the newspaper now serving the largest ecclesial jurisdiction in the United States.

In its ten decades, *The Tidings* has reported and recorded the flowering of the Church in a land where adobe missions and crude presidios once formed the frontier of Christendom.

As *The Tidings* observes its centennial of service, it is a basically healthy and well run newspaper. Though its circulation is down, its readership has held proportionately better than most of its sister newspapers in the country. And that says a lot about the product.

Oh, *The Tidings* is old, very old, and surely it will need some cosmetic surgery as it faces the challenge of the 21st century. But, what is old is noble; what is good is memorable and what is successful is imitable.

Perhaps it wouldn't be out of order to speak about the venerable paper in that context. After all, *The Tidings* is the longest continuously published Catholic newspaper on the west coast of America.

Consider these factors: (a) Because of the careful management of its resources, *The Tidings* paid its way and remained in the black during a crucial period when upwards of 85% of the Catholic papers in the United States needed to be subsidized;

(b) For almost forty years, *The Tidings*' building at 1530 West Ninth Street provided free rent for no fewer than eleven agencies which serve the People of God in the Archdiocese of Los Angeles;

(c) *The Tidings* quantitatively has won twenty-seven national and numerous regional awards, which is more than any other Catholic newspaper on the continent. And that says nothing about the dozens of citations bestowed by local civic and religious leaders;

(d) *The Tidings* has responded to the social needs of the past four decades by plowing more than $2,000,000 of its assets into the inner city's parishes and schools. *The Tidings* not alone preached the Gospel, it reached out to the poor and implemented its message;

And, finally, (e) Its remaining assets were used to establish *Vida Nueva*, a Catholic newspaper which has become the voice of the Church for the millions of Hispanic peoples now residing in the Archdiocese of Los Angeles.

The Tidings stands tall among its peers. It doesn't have to apologize to any other outreach program in the archdiocese. No Catholic paper in the country can boast of such accomplishments.

The "Grand Old Lady of the Catholic Press" is ready for the next century of its service to the Church in California's southland.

Appendix I
Locations of The Tidings

258 New High St. . . . . .June 29, 1895-June 6, 1896

Security and Bank Building
  2nd and Main Sts . . . . .June 6, 1896-Sept. 30, 1899

204 South Main St. . . . . .Oct. 7, 1899-April 8, 1904

206 South Main St. . . . . .Apr. 8, 1904-Oct. 21, 1904

600 H.W. Hellman Bldg. . . . . .Oct. 21, 1904-June 21, 1912

216 Higgins Bldg. . . . . .June 28, 1912-July 5, 1918

809 Higgins Bldg. . . . . .July 12, 1918-Apr. 14, 1922

831 Higgins Bldg. . . . . .Apr. 14, 1922-June 14, 1923

815 Higgins Bldg. . . . . .June 22, 1923-Jan. 9, 1925

611 Higgins Bldg. . . . . .Jan. 16, 1925-Feb. 18, 1927

623 Higgins Bldg. . . . . .Feb. 25, 1927-Sept. 7, 1929

130 E. Second St. . . . . .Oct. 2, 1929-Dec. 21, 1934

4163 South Broadway . . . . .Dec. 28, 1934-Jan. 1, 1938

3241 South Figueroa . . . . .Jan. 7, 1938-May 14, 1955

1530 West Ninth St. . . . . .May 15, 1955-Onwards

Appendix II
Mission Statement of
The Tidings – 1988

To publish a Catholic weekly newspaper for the Archdiocese of Los Angeles that reports news of the Church locally, nationally and universally. The focus of the news will be ecclesial, theological and religious. Aspects of secular news, of public policy issues affected by this focus will also be reported. Besides news, *The Tidings* also provides commentary from a Catholic viewpoint on public issues with a view to enabling Catholics to participate in an informed way in political, social and cultural issues. Columnists deal with social teaching, family life, liturgy, doctrine, entertainment and sports.

(1) To focus the coverage on the issues, events and persons pertaining to the mission of the Church.

(2) To inform and educate the readers on the doctrine of the Church, the teachings of the Holy Father and the instructions and policies of the American bishops and the local ordinary.

(3) To keep the Catholic families of the Archdiocese in touch with the thinking and actions of the Church.

(4) To inform national and international readers the news events of the largest Archdiocese in the country.

(5) To publish more news editorials which will enhance the appeal of the paper.

(6) To increase *The Tidings* circulation through:

   a. conducting the school campaign with the new feature of requiring a *Tidings* subscription as part of the admission procedures;

   b. initiating a parish plan mandated by the Archbishop utilizing the pulpit on *Tidings* Sunday, parish membership lists for direct appeal and purchasing subscriptions for the core leadership groups of the parish.

(7) To maintain a 60/40 mix between news and advertising.

(8) To survey a representative sample of pastors and school principals and parishioners on ways to improve *The Tidings*.

(9) To continue to use the National Catholic News Service as a source for publishing a quality newspaper.

(10) To conduct quarterly meetings of the Board of Directors for the following purposes:

a. Assessing advertising opportunities

b. reviewing the objectives

c. measuring their implementation.

Appendix III
"California's Catholic Heritage"

The following served as the "Preface" for a book entitled *California Catholic Essays* which appeared on the bookstores in mid 1994.

History is drama and the historian is a dramatist. His function is to make the past come alive in the present, thereby reenacting on the printed page the doings and misdoings of those who have passed from the center stage.

And, in the process, Francis Bacon reminds historians that "true office of history is to represent the events, themselves, leaving the observations and conclusions to the reader's judgment."

Those simple principles have served as guidelines for this writer since the first of the columns on "California's Catholic Heritage" began appearing in *The Tidings*, the official Catholic newspaper for the Archdiocese of Los Angeles, on April 5, 1963.

Who would have imagined that those essays would continue for thirty years, thus becoming the longest-running column ever printed in a Catholic newspaper in the United States!

Statistically, more than 1,724 columns have appeared over the past three decades. At approximately 600 words per article, that means that over 1,034,400 words have been written about the Catholic history of California in this series alone.

Readership response has been extensive and supportive over the years and attempts have been made (not always successfully) to answer each and every one of the letters sent to the Archival Center, even the relatively few that were critical.

This is the eleventh volume of those collected essays to appear in book form. The earlier titles were *Reading in California Catholic History* (1967), *Catholic Footprints in California* (1970), *The Pilgrim Church in California* (1973), *California's Catholic Heritage* (1974), *California Catholicism* (1975), *California Catholicity* (1979), *California, The Catholic Experience* (1981), *Vignettes of California Catholicism* (1988), *Golden State Catholicism* (1990), *Catholic California* (1992), and *California Catholic Essays* (1994).

In addition, two specialty series found their way into print. They are *America's Catholic Heritage* (1976) and *The Life and Times of Fray Junipero Serra* (1984). While the text of the original articles remained substantially unchanged, a number of stylistic alterations give this volume and its predecessors a more attractive and readable format.

The historical well is far from dry and each day provides additional pieces for the jigsaw puzzle comprising the Catholic story in California. Hopefully, when the mortician carts my earthly remains off to the local boneyard, a new, younger and more vibrant writer will take up the challenge of telling contemporary Catholics about their roots. The narrative will only be completed on judgment day.

Finally, I must confess that writing these essays has been considerably more fun than work. The late Cardinal Timothy Manning put it another way when he observed that "more than the farmer wants the milk, the cow wants to give it."

Appendix IV
"A Busy Day in the Life of an Editor"

The following essay appeared in the issue for June 29, 1990.

For the editor of *The Tidings*, a new week begins every Thursday morning. It's time for planning the following week's paper, assigning stories and responding to the flood of mail that streams into the news desk. The early afternoon is reserved for a staff meeting at which the skeleton of the next issue begins to take its shape.

There are some on-going projects that never end, first of which is the ticker tape which brings news items and stories from the Catholic News Service in Washington. Each article is scanned for possible relevance to the local scene. Special emphasis is placed on papal announcements and movements, together with activities and pronouncements of leading clerical and lay personages.

Friday usually provides an opportunity for writing *El Rodeo* or mapping out some other major article or coverage. Weekend assignments are handed out to the three staff writers on a rotational basis. We endeavor to cover all major Catholic events in the three county archdiocese. When that proves impossible, we contact one of our stringers at the local level.

More often than not, the editor covers one or more stories himself during the weekend, always carrying along his trusty Nikon camera. Weekends also provide an opportunity for telling people at the local level what *The Tidings* is all about and why it needs parochial support.

Monday and Tuesday are given over to writing and/or editing articles, together with proof-reading galleys that have returned by messenger from the printing plant in Carson. By early afternoon on Monday, one of the staff members has charted out which stories will appear and where.

On Tuesday morning, the director of advertising informs us about the size of the weekly paper. Page numbers are normally determined by the amount of ads, a reasonable mix for which is 60/40%. With the ads frozen into place by 10 o'clock, it becomes possible to visualize what the final paper will look like.

After faxing all the last minute corrections and late-breaking news events to the printer, the weary crew works well into Tuesday night.

On Wednesday morning, the editor, the associate editor and the director of advertising arrive at the Carson plant of Rodgers and McDonald Graphics at 6:30 a.m. By then the pages are roughly mocked up, usually with numerous overruns spilling into the gutters.

The mock-up is xeroxed and once again the whole issue is proofed. Final touches are put on the various articles and announcements. Not infrequently, last minute mini-stories are written. Mostly the emphasis is on cutting out materials rather than writing or adding.

As the pages gradually work into place, the paper slowly emerges into its final stage. About noon, the staff signs off and the paper is "put to bed."

And it is the evening of the seventh day.

Appendix V
Circulation Figures for
The Tidings

1942	10,000
1949	42,000
1951	50,000
1952	72,017
1959	90,000
1961	112,000
1962	107,876
1964	125,000
1966	120,356
1988	49,000
1994	27,000

Appendix VI
"Interim Editor's First and Last Editorial"

The following essay appeared in *The Tidings* for August 24, 1990.

Following a lecture I gave Sunday evening at Santa Ines Mission in Solvang, a youngish lady came up to me with what she called a "perplexing question."

"Why does the Catholic press print stories about priests (and bishops) which are unpleasant and even scandalous. Wouldn't it be better to overlook such stories altogether?"

Judging from our mail, this same query crosses the mind of many Catholic people who recall the Pauline exhortation that "certain things are better left unsaid."

My response to the lady's question is repeated here for the benefit of others who might be interested in how such incidents are handled at *The Tidings*. Certain stories are admittedly touchy, especially when they surround or involve religious figures. Yet, once an indiscretion (or whatever) becomes public, it must be dealt with. If ever there was a time when these matters could be quietly closeted away, that time is long past. We live in an informationally-sensitive society. There are no longer any secrets.

The Catholic press has an obligation to inform its readers about everything that touches upon the Church or its mission in the world. We dare not deny, downplay or avoid an event just because it's "sticky."

But we do endeavor, to the best of our ability, to report such events within the context of their occurrence. This is all the more necessary because the secular press often exaggerates or otherwise distorts events that involve religious personages or policies.

Maybe we should take it as a compliment that the press pays so much attention to the Catholic Church. As Fulton Sheen once observed, "If God's Church were not important, you can be sure that the world would ignore us."

When one of these "unpleasant" stories surfaces, at the national or international level, it is generally covered by the Catholic News Service. One of their writers then prepares a feature story for members subscribing to the CNS. Such stories are updated and expanded as additional factors unfold.

The editors of the diocesan newspapers determine whether they will use the CNS story or prepare their own at the local level.

Here at *The Tidings*, we try to keep our coverage "tight." We don't overdwell on the spectaculars of a given story, but rather we endeavor to present them objectively and fully.

We feel that Catholics should not have to read the *Los Angeles Times* or any other secular newspaper to find out what is happening to, in or about the Church.

And we want to make sure that our readers have the benefit of all the facts, not just those which make this or that story an attractive issue or a banner headline for the newsstands.

We are, by God's design, a human Church. To deny that humanity, to gloss over its presence or to minimize its weaknesses would be patently wrong. Ours is a pilgrim Church, mud-splashed with the passage of many centuries.

Percentage-wise, the Church of the 1990s is probably no better or worse than it was in apostolic times. Peter denied Christ, Thomas doubted Him and Judas betrayed Him.

And had the indiscretions of the apostles been hidden away, there would be no New Testament. It's all part of the salvation story!

Appendix VII
Editors of The Tidings
(1895-1995)

1.	Patrick W. Croake	June 29,1895-December 31, 1898
2.	John J. Bodkin	January 7, 1899-August 26, 1904
3.	Elmer Murphy	October 21, 1904-February 23, 1906
4.	Joseph D. Lynch	March 2, 1906-July 27, 1906
5.	John F. Byrne	June 29, 1906-July 27, 1906
6.	Herman J. Rodman	August 31, 1906-July 19, 1907
7.	Rev. John J. Clifford	July 26, 1907-July 12, 1908
8.	Alice J. Stevens	July 17, 1908-October 15, 1913
9.	Charles C. Conroy	October 15, 1913-December 31, 1925
10.	Rev. Thomas J. Gorman	January 1, 1926-May 22, 1931
11.	Rev. John Dunne	May 29, 1931-October 9, 1942
12.	Rev. Thomas McCarthy	October 9, 1942-July 15, 1949
13.	Msgr. William North	July 22, 1949-June 7, 1957
14.	Msgr. Patrick Roche	June 14, 1957-August 24, 1973
15.	Alphonse Antczak	August 31, 1973-September 29, 1989
16.	William Rivera	October 1, 1989-May 11, 1990
17.	Msgr. Francis Weber	May 18, 1990-August 24, 1990
18.	Alfred Doblin	August 31, 1990-May 8, 1992
19.	Tod Tamberg	May 15, 1992

Appendix VIII
Typical "El Rodeo" Column

The following essay, which appeared in *El Rodeo* for August 24th, 1990, gives an example of how the column was used at various times).

Each year, Hollywood's Motion Picture Industry formally and ceremoniously recognizes excellence within its ranks by singling out those associated with the production, distribution and orchestration of movies classics for distinctive honors.

Actual bestowal of the coveted Oscars is reserved for a specially staged awards banquet attended by the greats of the film colony. The elaborate program is beamed to an anxiously-expectant television audience scattered across the nation.

While there's often a ring of insincerity associated with the conferal of the Academy Awards, the basic idea of publicly expressing gratitude has much to recommend it – especially to Christians.

The followers of the Nazarene, above all others, should be ever alert for occasions on which to manifest publicly their gratitude to God for His many favors and blessings.

Perhaps that gratefulness could be proclaimed in a manner parallel to that used for the Academy Awards –

(1) As a mark of gratitude for an isolated achievement, they might designate, as the all-time best producer, God The Father, for His creativity, patience and concern on behalf of humankind;

(2) As a token of gratitude for an isolated achievement, they might cite, as the best leading-man, Jesus Christ, for His unequalled redemptive role;

(3) As a measure of gratitude for an ongoing achievement, they might proclaim, as the best director, the Holy Spirit, for His sustenance and guidance in daily life;

(4) As an expression of gratitude for an singular achievement, they might portray, as the best leading lady, the Blessed Virgin, for her cheerful and eager participation in the pageant of Bethlehem;

(6) As a sign of gratitude for heroic achievement, they might single out, as

the best supporting actress, Mary Magdalen, for her undivided love and limitless dedication to the Messiah;

(7) As a symbol of gratitude for a collective achievement, they might label, as the best production, the Catholic Church, for its unique position in salvation history;

(8) As an emblem of gratitude for a peerless achievement, they might nominate, as the best script, the Redemption of Humankind, for its 1990th consecutive year as "The Greatest Story Ever Told."

How long has it been since we publicly thanked Almighty God for the faith we profess, the food we consume, the families we love, the friends we have and the health we enjoy?

May it not be said that gratitude has become the least exploited of the natural virtues in this era of plenitude!

Appendix IX
Staff of The Tidings, 1995

David G. Moore, General Manager

Teresa Perez, Office Manager
Virgina Gomez, Secretary/Receptionist
Mary Ellen Rodriguez, Administrative Secretary

Tod Tamberg, *Tidings* Editor
Hermine Lees, Staff Reporter
Mike Nelson, Staff Reporter

Karen Steeb, Creative Director
John Chacon, Production Assistant
Mia Leonelli, Production Assistant
Morris Neer, Graphics Specialist
Sari Rodriguez, Production Assistant
Ricardo Silva, Production Assistant

Ed Alvarez, Director of Sales & Advertising
Celia Alvarez, Telemarketer
Suky DeBellis, 130Advertising Supervisor
Maria Rios, Classified Ads
Isabel Rodriguez, Telemarketer
Angelina Valenzuela, Sales Representative

Mary Trudeau-Mottola, Circulation/Promotions Manager
German Cortes, Circulation Representative
Jennie Williams, Circulation Representative

Polo Dias, Finance Officer
Ana Fernandez, Bookkeeper
Thersa Goldner, Bookkeeper
Cora Leauterio, Accountant
Ovidio Torres, Collections

Victor Aleman, *Vida Nueva* Editor
Rogelio Fojo, Staff Reporter
Alicia Morandi, Staff Reporter
Patricia Prieto, Staff Reporter
Roger Sanchez, Proofreader

Appendix X
The Tidings Board of Directors

Dr. David Hayes-Bautista

Mr. Tom Castro

Msgr. Terrance Fleming

Mr. George Gibbs

Msgr. Alfred Hernandez

Mr. James L. Hesburgh, Chairman

Mr. Walter Johnson

Cardinal Roger Mahony, President

Mr. David G. Moore

Mr. Peter O'Malley

Sr. Kathleen Reilly, C.S.C.

Ms. Estella Romero

Mr. W. Pendleton Tudor

Mrs. Helen Walsh

Most Reverend John Ward

Msgr. Francis J. Weber

Mr. Horace Williams